EXPLORING the RICHEST MINE

Harnessing the Power Within for Personal, Financial and Professional Success

Toyin Obafemi

Copyright 2024 by Toyin Obafemi

Published by Pnuxel Consulting
toyin@pnuxelconsulting.com

All rights reserved. No part of this book may be reproduced or transmitted in any form or by any means- electronic or mechanical, including photocopying, recording, or by any information storage and retrieval system without the author's written permission except for the inclusion of brief quotations in a review.

Contents

Acknowledgements v

Introduction 7

Chapter One: Unveiling the Riches Within 15
    Unveiling The Intricate Features Of The Mind 15
    1) The Mind Was Given To Us Freely 18
    2) The Mind Serves As The Most Powerful Creative Engine On Earth 22
    3) The Mind Has The Power Of Life And Death. As Much As It Can Be Engaged To Better Lives, It Can Also Be A Tool To Destroy. 26
    Nine Ways To Cultivate A Positive Mindset 42
    4) The Mind Holds The Power To Create Wealth . 52
    The Difference And Connection Between Knowledge, Understanding And Wisdom............. 60
    5) Sadly, It Is One Of The Most Underutilised Resources... 68

Chapter Two: The Gift of Time: Understanding Its Value and Converting It Into Success 77
    Time Is A Free Gift Given To Us............................... 84
    Managing Time Effectively And Efficiently........... 86
    A Structured Approach To Managing Your Time Effectively And Efficiently 94
    Can Time Be Bought? 104
    Saving And Investing Time For Success 109
    Remember: Time Can Be Wasted 118

Your Success Reflects Your Time Management... 125
Adopt A Sense Of Urgency Regarding Your Activities.. 128
Time Once Lost Cannot Be Regained: The Impact Of Personal Choices On Your Lifespan And Potential. 132
The Overlooked Treasure 136
Make The Most Of Every Chance You Get 138
Reflect, Adjust, and Take Action............................. 154

Chapter Three: The Power of Thoughts: Nothing Meaningful Happens Without It 157

Is It A Crime To Think?... 159
Embrace Your Divine Nature................................... 168
Would You Like To Earn More? 179
Thinkers And Strategists Are Paid More............... 192
The Physical World Is An Expression Of The Invisible World 198

Chapter Four: How to Leverage the Richest Mine 205

Automating Your Journey To Success 206
A Simple Guide On How To Leverage The Richest Mine. 209

Unlock Your Potential: Discover the Transformative Power of My Other Books 228

The Author 232

References 235

Acknowledgements

First and foremost, I want to express my heartfelt gratitude to the omnipotent God — the One with unlimited power and capacity — who, out of His benevolence, has blessed us to partake in His life, power, and wealth.

To my loving and caring wife, Temitope, thank you for your constant encouragement and unwavering support. Your belief in me serves as a powerful source of motivation. I am deeply grateful for you.

I would also like to appreciate our precious children, Oreofe and Inioluwa, for being a continual source of inspiration. Watching you grow has given me glimpses of how greatness unfolds. Your joy, peace, and curiosity remind me of the beauty of living in the present and making the most of every moment.

A special thank you to Adewobi Adebanjo for designing the cover of this book. Your creativity and reliability continue to be invaluable. I truly appreciate your efforts.

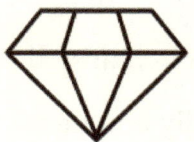

Introduction

"Wisdom provides solutions, and often, you are not compensated for your knowledge but for the solutions you offer."

One might naturally assume that the wealthiest nations are those abundantly endowed with mineral resources. However, this assumption often proves misleading. Take Africa, for instance, a continent blessed with a myriad of mineral riches. Despite the vast resources embedded in its soil, numerous African countries are referred to as developing or third-world nations. The paradox lies in the fact that the wealth within the earth's womb does not automatically translate into prosperity for the people. Picture a country blessed with petroleum, yet its citizens struggle to secure a dollar per day - the unemployment rate soars, underscoring the harsh reality that mineral abundance does not automatically equate to national prosperity.

This scenario underscores the multifaceted nature of wealth. Possessing mineral resources might just be the starting point. Unlocking the wealth in these resources requires knowledge, skill, and a strategic approach, which can be summed as wisdom.

> **Wisdom provides solutions, and often, you are not compensated for your knowledge but for the solutions you offer.**

For instance, ignorance about the mineral resources in the first place can leave a nation sitting on gold to grapple with poverty, and awareness of it without the know-how to extract and process the resources is equally limiting. Just as one of my sayings, "**Wisdom provides solutions, and often, you are not compensated for your knowledge but for the solutions you offer.**" Wisdom is crucial, highlighting that the richest mines are not necessarily the most recognised mineral deposits worldwide, like the Bingham Canyon Mine in the United States, which is the largest artificially made excavation in the world, or the Kimberley Diamond Mine in South Africa or the oil wells in Nigeria.

While writing this book, I came across a concept - the **resource curse,** also known as the **paradox of plenty**. It refers to the phenomenon wherein countries rich in natural resources, such as oil or minerals, often face adverse economic, social, and political consequences rather than enjoying the expected benefits.[1] This further emphasises that there is more to wealth than the endowment of mineral resources.

> **These nations exemplify the prowess of tapping into a different mine altogether—the human mind.**

Conversely, there are nations with minimal or no significant mineral resources that successfully transform their hardship into prosperity. **These**

Introduction

nations exemplify the prowess of tapping into a different mine altogether—the human mind.

For instance, Japan is a resource-poor nation with limited natural resources. It is referred to as a mountainous, volcanic island country with inadequate natural resources to support its growing economy and large population. However, Japan transformed itself into an economic powerhouse. Japan's success can be attributed to its emphasis on technological innovation and high-quality manufacturing.[2-4]

This leads us to ask, 'Where does one find the richest mine on Earth?' Is it nestled beneath the vast landscapes of Africa, Asia, North America, or South America? The surprising truth is that the wealthiest mine isn't a remote location on a map; it is nestled within every one of

> **While continents may boast of rich mineral resources, none compare to the treasure trove of ideas, creativity, resilience, and untapped capabilities that reside within the confines of our minds.**

10

us – our minds. **While continents may boast of rich mineral resources, none compare to the treasure trove of ideas, creativity, resilience, and untapped capabilities that reside within the confines of our minds.**

The most invaluable asset resides within the confines of our minds, waiting to be mined. The mind emerges as the most important mine, transcending the limitations of finite resources. **Without the ability to mine the treasure within your mind, you risk languishing in poverty and unfulfillment.**

Picture this: your mind, a mine not of rocks and minerals but a collection of your greatest assets, given freely to you. It is one of those precious gifts we often overlook, whereas it is the most significant mine waiting to be explored. The mind stands as an unparalleled source of riches, yet it's a resource frequently undervalued and underutilised.

> **Without the ability to mine the treasure within your mind, you risk languishing in poverty and unfulfillment.**

Consider this irony: some of the most valuable things are usually given to us freely but are often the least appreciated. Our minds, gifted without a price tag, are entrusted with the potential to shape our destinies.

> *"The mind is not a vessel to be filled, but a fire to be kindled," - the ancient philosopher Plutarch.*

The world often clamours for physical wealth and therefore discounts the very mine within us because it is intangible – though intangible, it holds the power to create the best we could ever imagine in the physical world. Our minds, if priced, would surpass any commodity, for they hold the key to unlocking our true potential. Time, another invaluable resource freely bestowed upon us, parallels this concept. Imagine if time were a commodity traded in the marketplace – its value is immeasurable, but many people do not acknowledge this.

In the sections and chapters ahead, we'll delve deeper into the treasures hidden within our minds, recognising them as the true riches that can shape our lives and help us fulfil our destinies. We will also consider how to leverage our minds for personal, financial, and professional success. Join me in uncovering the wealth within – the most precious mine on Earth, waiting to be explored.

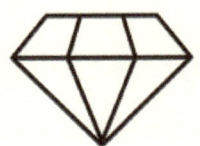

Chapter One

Unveiling the Riches Within

"Whatever the mind of man can conceive and believe, it can achieve." — Napoleon Hill

Unveiling The Intricate Features Of The Mind

As we start our journey into "Exploring the Richest Mine," we must first focus on some fundamental features of the mind that make it an extraordinary treasure trove.

First, we need to know that the mind was given to us freely by God, and within this divine gift lies the most potent creative engine on Earth. When harnessed, it is a force that can sculpt the most intricate dreams into reality. **Our minds are not mere recipients of external stimuli; they are active creators, capable of shaping worlds and moulding destinies.** This book aims to tap into the power within each of us for personal, financial, and professional success, ultimately contributing to the betterment of the world. The world eagerly awaits our unique expressions as we hold in our custody ideas that can make the earth a better place to live. Each one of us is unique, bestowed with a gift to share with the world. Let us not deprive the world of this gift by neglecting to engage the most creative engine in the world – the mind, a divine gift bestowed upon us by the Creator.

As much as the mind is an incredible creative engine, it carries a dual nature – it possesses the power of life and death. As we navigate the sections ahead, we'll explore the delicate balance between using the mind as a tool for empowerment and the potential pitfalls of allowing it to become a force of destruction. It is a reminder that the mind, though a beacon of creativity, requires mindful navigation to channel its energy positively.

As explained in Napoleon Hill's "Think and Grow Rich," the mind is not just a collection of thoughts; it is the birthplace of wealth. As was said in the book, **wealth and poverty are offsprings of the mind.** You can choose which of the two you want. In this book, we will look into how our thoughts and beliefs can shape our financial lives.

For all its grandeur, the mind is one of the most underutilised resources. Despite its divine origin and vast capabilities, the mind often remains a dormant force, waiting to be awakened. *"The mind is not a vessel to be filled, but a fire to be kindled,"* said the ancient philosopher Plutarch, illustrating our duty to our minds.

As we explore the features of the mind, remember that the power to shape your realities lies within you. The mind, given freely to you, **is not a silent observer of life but a co-author of your destiny.**

1) THE MIND WAS GIVEN TO US FREELY

In the creation narrative, a divine board meeting occurred among the Godhead to fashion a unique and extraordinary creation called man. Unlike previous creative endeavours, this assembly signified man's exceptional nature, requiring meticulous creativity and time to sculpt him into an excellent product.

Remarkably, everything else on earth was created for this product called man and not vice versa. *The Earth, the sun, the moon, trees, flowers, fishes, and all other elements were designed with man in mind.* Little wonder Apostle Paul exclaimed that God knew us before the earth's foundation; we existed before the Earth was created. This revelation is nothing short of inspiring. I didn't fully grasp what Paul meant until I understood the concept of the two creations, which we will delve into in the course of this book. Everything that was created underwent the process of creation twice—whether it's the sun, the moon, chairs, cars, or any other entity.

When God created the light or animals, for instance, He simply declared, *'Let there be light,'* and *'Let the earth produce living creatures according to their kinds,'* and it was so.[5-7] However, when it came to man, a unique process unfolded. Figuratively describing this process - when it came to the creation of man, God summoned the directors in charge, saying, *'Let us create man in our own image and likeness.'*[8] It's as if there is a corporation in heaven with a board of directors, and these directors had to convene for a meeting to create this new product- the earth had not seen anything like it before.

Do you know that you are unique and special, and the earth had not seen anything like you before you were created? This realisation should ignite an outstanding self-esteem within you as you fulfil the reason for your existence and bring meaning to those around you. You possess gifts meant to enrich your world - you have got gifts for the world. Would you tug your head in pity or raise your shoulders in confidence and self-esteem as you achieve the greatness you were meant for?

The approach in creating man involved innovation and purposeful planning — defining what the product would look like and what it would accomplish. The meeting's outcome was the blueprint for the production process to create man. They worked on their plan, as we saw in the creation of the human spirit and the moulding of his body so that he could interact with the physical world. Little wonder Pierre Teilhard de Chardin said, *"We are not human beings having a spiritual experience. We are spiritual beings having a human experience."*

Yet, a crucial aspect demands attention. Since they decided what the product should be and what it should do, they needed to provide the resources to achieve this purpose.

"What did they intend the product to be and do?" you may ask.

They said, *'Let us create man in our own image and likeness.'*[8] This means they wanted the new product to be like themselves. If there is anything we know about the Godhead up to the time of creating man, it is that they were creators. The opening statement of the Bible says, *'In the beginning, God created the heavens and the earth.'*[9] This shows that God is a creator. So, if the new product will take after their likeness, they must likewise be a creator. This reveals that man was created to be a creator, and any man who does not create is living below the standard and purpose for their existence. This is revealing! What do you think?

Now, take one to two minutes to ask yourself what was given to man to be like God as a creator.

What is your answer?

Are you able to come up with something?

Here is what he gave man to be a creator: the mind. God freely gave the human race the mind as a priceless gift for creating anything they desire. Although freely given, the mind plays a pivotal role in accomplishing the essence of man's existence. Unfortunately, this priceless gift is often undervalued and underutilised. This book aims to raise awareness and guide you to explore the greatest and richest mine — the mind — for personal, financial, and professional success and to benefit the world around you. Imagine a world where everyone puts their minds into creative mode to solve problems. Can you imagine how pleasant the world would be?

2) THE MIND SERVES AS THE MOST POWERFUL CREATIVE ENGINE ON EARTH

We have seen that we were created in the likeness and image of God. Deepak Chopra, author of The Seven Spiritual Laws of Success, articulated, *'In reality, we are divinity in disguise. True success is the unfolding*

of the divinity within us.' We were created to be creators, just as the Divine is a Creator. The Divine has given us what we need to shape our world, which is nothing but our minds. The mind serves as the most creative engine in the world, the yard for the manufacturing of ideas.

The astonishing things you see around you were birthed in some people's minds before they came into being. There is nothing we cannot do if we can think about it. Little wonder it is said that ***"if you can think it, then you can do it"***. When an idea comes to your mind, it is a testament that you can bring it to fruition. Do not be afraid to ideate, innovate, and work on your ideas — this is what you were created for. You were designed to be a co-creator with God.

Imagine living a century ago, and you were told you could communicate with someone on another continent, thousands of kilometres away, with just a few clicks. You wouldn't have believed it because, at that time, you probably couldn't even conceive it. But as people began to think about it, it became possible. While I do not know what the world will be like in years to come, I am sure that the future generation will wonder how we survived because our world might look too obsolete for them.

I once worked with a boss who narrated the ordeal they went through to exchange information across distance. When his wife was pregnant, he worked in the northern part of the country, hundreds of kilometres away. It took days to exchange messages — sometimes, they had to find someone, give the individual a letter, and then the person travelled all the way to deliver the message. His wife could not reach out to him when it was time to deliver their first child. Around that time, he had an instinct to travel home. If he hadn't, it would have taken days for him to get the information that his first child had been delivered. This wasn't as many years ago as you might think. Things changed because people thought of a solution; they created the solution. Now, in seconds, you can reach out to anyone, anywhere in the world, in real-time. This is the power of creativity.

Edison designed a product called 'Ediphone' and wanted to sell it. However, his sales team thought it wouldn't work out and rejected his idea. Edison conceived the idea, but his sales team could not embrace it. Many times, our minds create ideas that defy conventional culture and traditions. Edwin Barnes embraced the idea, and the product sales became a success.

Innovation usually challenges the status quo. We won't be better and more creative if we are not inquisitive.

A Bible story demonstrates how humans decided to build a tower that reached the heavens. They came together and started the work. They thought about it, innovated and got to work. This was a time when there was no sophisticated machinery, yet that could not stop what they had conceived. It was like building a skyscraper without the cranes, cement, rods, and other machinery used in our day. God had to confuse them with diverse languages, or else they would have achieved their plans. This demonstrates the creative energy and power of the mind. The mind is very innovative and holds the power to change our lives. If you want to change your life, then change the way you think because the mind is the most potent creative engine in the world.

This book will explore how to take advantage of this astounding creative engine.

3) The Mind Has The Power Of Life And Death. As Much As It Can Be Engaged To Better Lives, It Can Also Be A Tool To Destroy.

So far, we've explored two intricate features of the mind. First, we have established that the mind is a divine gift freely given to us by God. Despite its immeasurable value in shaping our lives and the world, it's often undervalued and underutilised. Second, we acknowledged the mind as Earth's most powerful creative engine, unparalleled in its ability to generate innovation. It's the driving force behind explorations around us, be it that of the seas, the deep, the skies, or outer space. The mind serves as the birthplace of these groundbreaking ideas. Now, having established that every human is a creator endowed with this essential tool, the mind, it's time to delve into the third intricate feature: the mind possesses the power of life and death. As much as it can be engaged to better lives, it can also be a tool to destroy.

From history, it is clear that the mind played a pivotal role in creating innovations that made life easy and at the same time, it was engaged in exploring ways to destroy lives. For instance, the use of nuclear substances showed how the knowledge and exploration in this field can be used to make life better or destroy humanity.

Through innovations of the mind, we learned how to use atoms to make nuclear weapons that can cause massive destruction. This dark side of the mind shows how bad intentions and selfish goals can lead to terrible things. In this case, the mind ushered in death, fear and harm.

On the other hand, when our intentions are good and we want to improve the world, that same nuclear substance becomes a force for progress and prosperity. The creative mind imagined a world where atomic energy could power our cities, light up our homes, and help us progress. Nuclear power stations, created through human innovation, show how the mind can be a force for good. In this way, the mind becomes a helper of life, giving energy to communities and making the society better.

This illustration reminds us that our minds have the power to create things that either help or harm. It is, therefore, our responsibility to use our minds for the good of everyone. The power of life and death is in our minds; the outcome depends on our choices and what we want to achieve.

Little wonder the wise King Solomon admonishes us to ***guard our hearts with all diligence, for out of them spring the issues of life.***[10] We have some lessons to learn from this wisdom. First, we are to guard our hearts with all diligence. Here, "heart" refers to our mind, not the organ that pumps blood throughout our bodies. We do not think with our literal hearts; instead, they pump blood to ensure that every cell of our bodies is nourished and cleansed. The Contemporary English Version sheds a better light on this verse, stating, ***"Carefully guard your thoughts because they are the source of true life."*** So, you are to guard your thoughts carefully, and we know that the seat of thoughts is the mind. This means you have a task concerning your mind: you are supposed to guard it.

Why Should You Guard Your Thoughts?

1. **You are to guard your thoughts because there are vices against them.** There is no need to guard something if there is no threat or onslaught against it. Just as you fortify your

homes against intruders, you must safeguard your thoughts from negative influences and harmful ideologies.

In some African stories, people would leave their goods in the market with stones to denote the prices, returning later to find them untouched and payment made in full. While this story reflects a sense of communal trust and honesty, it's impractical in our modern world, where individuals with ulterior motives seek to exploit vulnerabilities. Therefore, you mustn't leave your mind to chance or the mercy of thieves and robbers of our peace and well-being. By guarding your thoughts, you protect yourself from harmful external influences.

2. **Your thoughts often shape your actions and decisions.** Just as gardeners tend their gardens to ensure healthy growth, you must cultivate your thoughts to produce positive outcomes. Consider a garden overrun by weeds; if left

unchecked, these weeds can choke out the flowers and vegetables, hindering growth and beauty. Similarly, unchecked negative thoughts can overshadow your potential for success and fulfilment. As the bible aptly says, *"As a man thinketh in his heart, so is he."* By guarding your thoughts, you can ensure that your actions align with your goals and values.

3. **Your actions and attitude shape you.** Now that you have seen that your thoughts shape your actions and decisions. Do not forget that your actions and attitudes shape you. So, you need to guard your thoughts if you want to achieve the kind of success you want. You may not find a perfect environment to thrive in; however, you can create a productive one for yourself so that your actions are not influenced by what is happening around you but by your prevailing and burning desires to achieve greatness. It is true that you are what you think because your

thoughts influence your actions, and your actions define your life. Therefore, you cannot afford not to guard your thoughts with all diligence. I think your most important task is to guard your thoughts. If you are able to maintain positive thoughts, every other thing will fall into place.

4. **Your thoughts greatly influence your emotions and overall mental health.** Imagine if pests were left unchecked on your farm – they will destroy the crops. Similarly, harmful or toxic thoughts can lead to feelings of anxiety, depression, and despair. You can protect your emotional well-being and maintain inner peace by guarding your thoughts. As Viktor Frankl, the renowned psychiatrist and Holocaust survivor, wrote, *"Between stimulus and response, there is a space. In that space is our power to choose our response. In our response lies our growth and our freedom."* You can choose your response and

maintain good emotions and mental health by guarding your thoughts.

5. **Your thoughts affect your relationship with yourself.** Your thoughts profoundly influence how you relate, perceive, and value yourself, ultimately shaping your self-esteem. **Do you know that you are either your best friend or your worst enemy?** You decide if you are a friend or foe to yourself by your relationship with yourself which is fostered by your prevailing thoughts about yourself.

Imagine a mirror reflecting your inner dialogue; if filled with self-criticism and doubt, then it will result in self-pity, fear and self-doubt. Conversely, when your thoughts are kind and affirming, it leads to confidence and self-assurance. Your self-esteem is like a fragile seed; it requires nurturing and positive reinforcement to flourish. You can foster a healthy sense of self-esteem by guarding your thoughts and cultivating self-compassion and self-love. As Nathaniel Branden aptly said, *"Self-esteem is the reputation we acquire with ourselves."*

Your self-esteem, identity and self-image are the foundation upon which you build your personal, financial, and professional endeavours. Imagine a skyscraper soaring into the sky; its strength and stability rely on a solid foundation. Similarly, your self-esteem, identity and self-image provide the stability and resilience needed to navigate life's challenges and pursue your goals. You approach opportunities and failures with confidence and determination when you believe in yourself and your abilities. I hope you know that failure is a part of success, unlike what you were taught in school, so you need good self-esteem and the right self-identity to manoeuvre through failure and success.

6. **Your thoughts do not only affect your relationship with yourself but also with others.** Picture a delicate thread connecting two individuals; if frayed or weakened by negative thoughts, it can strain the bond between them. The little disagreements that occur among once-upon-a-time love birds, culminating in divorce, do not arise in a day; instead, they result from a series of thoughts harboured over time. These thoughts can transform love into hatred, attraction into resentment, trust into mistrust, and intimacy into a thing of the past. Guarding your thoughts is essential to maintaining healthy relationships and connections with the people around you.

7. **Your thoughts play a significant role in shaping your reality and manifesting your goals and dreams.** Just as a potter shapes the clay, so do your thoughts mould your life. By guarding your thoughts and maintaining a

positive mindset, you can align your thoughts with your aspirations and take inspired action towards achieving them. As Napoleon Hill famously stated, *"Whatever the mind can conceive and believe, it can achieve."*

Energy and matter are said to be the same but expressed in different forms. Your thoughts serve as the energy that can be transformed into tangible and physical matter. Therefore, holding onto negative thoughts and energy is unwise, as they have the potential to transform into their material form.

8. **Do you want to maintain clarity and focus? If yes, then you need to guard your thoughts.** The modern world bombards you with constant information and distractions, making it easy to lose sight of your priorities and goals. Imagine a calm lake; when undisturbed, the water is clear, and the reflections are sharp, but it could be muddy if disturbed. Similarly, you can

preserve your mental clarity and focus by guarding your thoughts and minimising distractions. This enables you to make informed decisions, solve problems effectively, and stay committed to your goals.

Now that we have explored why you should guard your thoughts, we are confronted with another question.

Have you asked what you should guard your thoughts from?

Have you?

If not, then take a minute to ask yourself, "What exactly am I supposed to guard my thoughts from?

> **You are the product of your prevailing thoughts.**

How can you guard or protect your mind if you do not know what you are protecting it from? It is essential to understand your adversary, their power, and the havoc they can wreak so that you know how to prepare and to what extent you should prepare. You do not have to overthink it; it's simple — you are to guard your thoughts from negative thoughts. It's a battle of thoughts. Your greatest warfare is right in your mind.

You are the product of your prevailing thoughts. While you cannot prevent negative thoughts from passing through your mind, you can prevent them from taking control or dominating your mind. As Kenneth E. Hagin popularly said, *"You cannot stop a bird from flying over your head, but you can stop it from building a nest on your head."* Therefore, be aware that, whether you like it or not, negative thoughts will come your way, but it is your responsibility not to allow them to take root in your mind. Just as weeds require little effort to grow abundantly, negative thoughts thrive effortlessly. Conversely, nurturing positive thoughts requires effort, just like cultivating and tending a valuable plant. Positive thoughts will enrich your life and lead you to success.

Why Should You Not Guard Alone But Guard Your Thoughts With All Diligence?

In the admonition of King Solomon, we are urged to guard our hearts with all diligence. But why the emphasis on diligence? This is because as a man thinketh in his heart, so is he.[11] Your entire essence depends on your thoughts. **Your thoughts shape your perceptions, decisions, and actions, ultimately determining the course of your lives.**

I love the New Living Translation's narration, which says, *"Guard your heart above all else, for it determines the course of your life."*[10] You can see that your prevailing thoughts determine the course and direction of your life. You cannot go away or opposite your thoughts. Therefore, you should change your thoughts if you want to change the course of your life. It is as simple as that because your mind serves as the steering or rudder for your life. Can you see why you should not joke about what takes prevalence in your thoughts? Can you see why you are not supposed just to guard but to guard your mind with diligence?

Your success, fulfilment, happiness or even otherwise hinges greatly on the quality of your thoughts. Weeds do not need to be planted or nurtured before they take over a piece of land- they grow effortlessness. This can be likened to negative thoughts. Negative thoughts, like weeds in a garden, can quickly overrun your mind if left unchecked. They can choke out positivity, hinder growth, and lead you astray from your goals. In today's world, negative influences abound. From the constant stream of negative news on television and social media to the complaints and grievances of those around you, it's easy to be overwhelmed with pessimism and unnecessary fear. Since negative thoughts abound, then you need diligence in mounting a protective wall against it. **You do not have to do**

anything to grow negative thoughts but you have got work to do to grow a positive mindset.

Diligence is necessary because it takes a concerted effort to maintain a positive mindset amidst the onslaught of negativity. Unlike weeds that flourish effortlessly, nurturing positive thoughts requires intentional cultivation and perseverance. It requires feeding your mind and thoughts with positive information and filtering those that weigh you down and dampen your spirit. Just as a gardener consistently nurtures and removes weeds in their garden, you should diligently grow your thoughts positively.

> **You do not have to do anything to grow negative thoughts, but you have got work to do to grow a positive mindset.**

In one of my books, **"Leveraging the Power of Seasons,"** I expound on the seven keys to recognising and taking advantage of opportunities, with the first key being Maintaining a Positive Mindset. This highlights the significance of maintaining a positive mindset. Therefore, let us delve into Nine Ways to Cultivate a Positive Mindset, which is crucial for personal, financial, and professional success.

NINE WAYS TO CULTIVATE A POSITIVE MINDSET

The first key to recognising and seizing opportunities, undoubtedly the most crucial, is cultivating a positive mindset. This key lays the foundation upon which all other keys to success rely. If you stumble at this initial step, the effectiveness of every other key diminishes. I would go as far as to say that a positive mindset is the master key to unlocking the doors of opportunity in your life.

The journey to changing your life for the better starts within – in your mind. You cannot experience a positive change without, without a positive change within. You don't necessarily need to alter the external circumstances surrounding you; instead, you should focus on changing your mindset. **The term "mindset" implies that the "mind" can be "set", much like how**

concrete solidifies. Consequently, changing a set mind demands a consistent and purposeful effort. It's no wonder that the wisdom of Solomon advises us to "guard our heart with all diligence, for out of it springs the issues of life," and in another translation, it says, *"Guard your heart above all else, for it determines the course of your life."* Protecting your mind and controlling what gains access to it requires diligence, and it is a worthy endeavour because your life inevitably follows the direction of your thoughts - your thoughts determine the course of your life. In essence, you are your thoughts. Therefore, cultivating a positive mindset is essential to recognise and seize opportunities.

> **The term "mindset" implies that the "mind" can be "set", much like how concrete solidifies. Consequently, changing a set mind demands a consistent and purposeful effort.**

To delve deeper into this concept, it's vital to understand that a positive mindset doesn't mean denying the existence of challenges. Instead, it's about maintaining an attitude that empowers you to overcome obstacles, learn from setbacks, and see the potential for growth in every situation. It's the ability to view difficulties as opportunities in disguise.

A positive mindset is like sunshine after a rainy day; it brightens everything. It's about believing in yourself and your abilities. When you wake up, tell yourself that great opportunities await you.

This mindset is a filter, helping you see the good in every situation. For example, if you face a setback at work, a positive attitude will allow you to see it as a chance to learn and grow. So, start each day with a smile, and you'll be surprised how vast opportunities will come your way.

> *"When one door of happiness closes, another opens; but often we look so long at the closed door that we do not see the one which has been opened for us." – Helen Keller*

Cultivating a positive mindset is akin to a farmer tending to his fields. Your mind serves as the fertile soil, and reaping its benefits necessitates a process of cultivation—beginning with soil preparation, sowing seeds, tending the crop, and weeding out weeds before the harvest. Clearly, this isn't a day's job; it involves weeks and even months of dedicated effort. However, it is an endeavour that reaps rich rewards. Now, let's explore nine ways to cultivate a positive mindset.

> You may be just one book away from your breakthrough.

1. **Read impactful books:** Engage with literature that has the potential to transform your life. **You may be just one book away from your breakthrough.** Establishing a habit of reading impactful books is of paramount importance. Your solution might be concealed within the pages of a book authored by someone who faced similar challenges in the past. Reading can save you years of trial and error. By delving into

the insights and strategies these authors share, you gain the advantage of standing on the shoulders of those who have come before you. This is undeniably one of the key ways to cultivate a positive mindset.

2. **Listen to impactful teachings:** Similar to reading books, actively engaging with impactful audio content, such as podcasts and audiobooks, among others, is essential.

Research from Harvard University found that the average American adult spends an average of 101 minutes driving daily.[12,13] Based on Harvard's figures, the average commuter could listen to almost 50 extra books in a year since many audiobooks are under eight hours long.[12,14] Can you imagine what your life would look like if you could listen to 50 books in one year?

3. **Surround Yourself with Positive People:** Spend time with people who uplift and inspire you. The people around you rub on you and emit energies that can impact you positively or otherwise. So you want positive people around you as this will help you cultivate positive mindsets.

4. **Set short and long-term goals:** Setting goals is a fundamental key to cultivating a positive mindset because it provides a clear sense of purpose and direction. When you set meaningful goals, you give yourself something to strive for, which can be incredibly motivating. This sense of purpose and motivation inherently fosters positivity because it shifts your focus from dwelling on problems or uncertainties to actively working toward solutions and growth.

Moreover, setting goals helps you envision a better future, a cornerstone of a positive mindset. By defining what you want to achieve, you paint a mental picture of success, and this visualisation can serve as a powerful source of inspiration and optimism. As you progress toward your goals, even small steps forward can boost your confidence and reinforce the belief that you have control over your destiny. It's not just about reaching the end goal but also about the journey and personal growth that occurs along the way, which can significantly contribute to a positive and empowered mindset. In essence, setting and pursuing goals provide structure to your life and infuse it with a sense of purpose and optimism.

5. **Practice Gratitude:** Regularly expressing appreciation for the good things in your life, no matter how small they may seem, helps you put on a positive mindset even when things are not going how you want.

6. **Embrace Failure:** One of the essential keys to cultivating a positive mindset is to embrace

> **Failure is part of winning and not the opposite of winning.**

failure as a natural part of the journey toward success. The journey to success is not a straight line; it is curvy with mountains and valleys and, of course, pastures along the way.

Failures are not setbacks but stepping stones to growth and resilience. As the legendary basketball player Michael Jordan once said, *"I've missed more than 9,000 shots in my career. I've lost almost 300 games. Twenty-six times, I've been trusted to take the game-winning shot and missed. I've failed over and over and over again in my life. And that is why I succeed."*

Embracing failure means learning from mistakes, adapting, and persisting despite setbacks. It recognises that every stumble brings you closer to your goals, as Winston Churchill noted: "*Success is not final, failure is not fatal: It is the courage to continue that counts.*" When you view failure as a valuable teacher rather than an adversary, you nurture a positive mindset that thrives on resilience, perseverance, and the unwavering belief that setbacks are inscribed into the path to success.

It is good to know that **failure is part of winning and not the opposite of winning.**

7. **Embrace the Present. Let Go of the Past:** Another essential key to cultivating a positive mindset is to free yourself from the shackles of the past. Dwelling on past mistakes, regrets, or missed opportunities can weigh heavily on your psyche and hinder your ability to seize new opportunities in the present. As Eckhart Tolle wisely noted, "*Realise deeply that the present moment is all you ever have.*" Embracing the present moment allows you to fully engage with your current circumstances and

possibilities, unburdened by the baggage of the past.

8. **Limit Exposure to Negativity:** Another crucial key to cultivating a positive mindset is limiting exposure to negativity, which includes reducing consumption of negative news, media, and influences that bring you down. In a world of constant information, it's essential to filter out sources that perpetuate negativity and focus on what uplifts and inspires. Remember, you can curate your media intake, ensuring it aligns with your goals and values. Doing so creates a mental environment conducive to nurturing positivity, enabling you to seize opportunities with a renewed sense of optimism.

9. **Celebrate Small Wins:** Acknowledge and celebrate your achievements, no matter how minor they may seem, as it is also pivotal to cultivating a positive mindset. Rejoicing in the little victories along the way matters.

As Mark Twain stated, *"The secret of getting ahead is getting started."* No matter how small, each step propels you forward and validates your efforts. By acknowledging and appreciating these incremental achievements, you boost your self-esteem and have a cheerful disposition to life even if you have not gotten what you wanted. Remember that accumulating these small victories gives room to the so-called big success. As Robert Collier wisely said, *"Success is the sum of small efforts repeated day in and day out."* The small wins ultimately lead to grand triumphs.

Explore the richest mine by cultivating a positive mindset as we have discussed.

4) THE MIND HOLDS THE POWER TO CREATE WEALTH

So far, we have explored three intricate features of the mind. Firstly, we discovered that the mind is a gift from God, intended to aid you in fulfilling your life's purpose. Following this, we explored its role as a powerful creative engine responsible for birthing innovations and achieving remarkable feats. Just before this moment, we examined the dual nature of the mind: it serves as both a transformer and a destroyer. This paradox highlights the importance of how we engage this powerful entity, as it can either contribute to the betterment of humanity or become a source of destruction. Recognising the profound impact the mind has on our lives, we concluded the section by outlining nine ways to maintain a positive mindset.

> **Your mind holds the power to generate wealth.**

As we continue our discussion, here is another remarkable feature of the mind: its inherent capacity to create wealth. Beyond what we have explored thus far, **the mind holds the power to generate wealth.** Every individual who has amassed wealth has engaged their mind in this pursuit. Napoleon Hill's popular book, 'Think and Grow Rich,' extensively expounds on the mind's ability to create wealth. As aptly stated in the book, *'Wealth and poverty are both offspring of the mind.'* This implies that whether you become wealthy or impoverished depends on how you have engaged your mind.

Numerous success stories throughout history exemplify the mind's capacity to create wealth. Consider the story of Thomas Edison, whose inventive mind led to the creation of the electric light bulb, revolutionising the world and amassing great wealth in the process. Edison famously stated, *"Genius is one percent inspiration and ninety-nine per cent perspiration."* This shows the importance of running with the idea generated by your mind until you transform the energy in your mind into matter. As we have seen that, all things exist either as energy or matter. We have also seen that **energy and matter are the same thing, existing in different forms.** This

> **Energy and matter are the same thing, existing in different forms.**

means your thought is in the "energy state," which can be transformed into its physical "matter state" through faith, courage and persistence.

It is no secret that people are naturally drawn to value. Wealth gravitates towards individuals who provide solutions to problems. Problem solvers become wealthy because people are willing to pay for the solutions they offer. After all, why would anyone willingly part with their hard-earned money for nothing? Money flows in the direction of value creation, and the primary vehicle for creating value and solutions is the mind. This underscores the profound capacity of the mind to generate wealth. As Jim Rohn famously said, *'You get paid for bringing value to the marketplace.'* Therefore, those who leverage their minds to innovate and provide valuable solutions are aptly rewarded with financial abundance.

> **People are naturally drawn to value. Wealth gravitates towards individuals who provide solutions to problems.**

However, recognising that wealth extends beyond mere monetary riches is important. True wealth encompasses various aspects of life, including health. It's noteworthy that maintaining a positive mindset is closely linked to overall well-being. Numerous studies have shown that individuals with a positive outlook on life tend to enjoy better physical health, increased longevity, and greater resilience in the face of adversity.[15-17] This highlights the intrinsic connection between mindset and health, emphasising the holistic nature of wealth.

Wealth transcends the mere accumulation of money and extends beyond material possessions. While the poor may chase after money and the rich after accumulating material things, the truly wealthy pursue ideas. The wealthy understand that true value creation stems from innovative ideas that better the lives of others. Rather than solely focusing on personal gain, they strive to make life better and easier for people, knowing that the accumulation of fortune is a natural by-product of their generosity.

There are different forms of wealth - spiritual, soulic, physical, social, community, and generational wealth. Wealth is more than the accumulation of riches; it is much more about your legacy and impact on the people around you. As Billy Graham aptly put it, *'The legacy we leave is not just in our possessions, but in the quality of our lives.'*

Looking at the different forms of wealth, an individual can be wealthy in one area while lacking in another; for instance, someone may accumulate vast material wealth, which can be referred to as physical wealth, but have poor social relationships, rendering them impoverished regarding social wealth. Therefore, pursuing true wealth entails striving for abundance in all spheres of wealth, focusing on making a positive impact and leaving a lasting legacy.

As we have seen, the mind holds the capacity to create wealth. How we engage our minds determines the extent of our success in achieving wealth in its various forms. This echoes the sentiment of Napoleon Hill, who wrote in his book *Think and Grow Rich*, *'The starting point of all achievement is desire. Keep this constantly in mind. Weak desire brings weak results, just as a small fire makes a small amount of heat.'* Therefore, cultivating a positive mindset is paramount, as it serves as the cornerstone for unleashing the mind's creative potential and manifesting wealth across its dimensions.

In essence, true wealth is measured not by the riches you amass but by the value you create, the lives you touch, and the legacy you leave behind. By embracing these principles of value creation, selflessness, and generosity, you can cultivate wealth in its truest sense.

> *'You can have everything in life you want if you will just help enough other people get what they want.'* -
> *Zig Ziglar,*

Therefore, let us strive to be wealthy in all spheres of life, driven by a positive mindset and a commitment to making a meaningful difference in the world.

> *"Whether you think you can, or you think you can't — you're right,"* -
> *Henry Ford*

You are at par with the quality of your thoughts. Hill emphasises the importance of a burning desire, faith, and persistence in achieving wealth. He asserts that a burning desire, combined with unwavering faith in one's ability to attain wealth, can unleash the creative forces of the mind.

When you pray for wealth, God will answer you by teaching you how to create wealth. He will not rain money from heaven, but He will answer your prayers by giving you ideas that will catapult you into the kind of abundance and wealth you desire. Just as it was well said in the Bible, *"And you shall remember the LORD your God,* **for it is He who gives you power to get wealth,** *that He may establish His covenant which He swore to your fathers, as it is this day."*[18]

I wrote a book recently titled **"FROM DEBT TO WEALTH. 12 Keys To Earn Money With What You Have"**. You can get it here: https://www.amazon.co.uk/dp/B0DGMD6HHP, or check any of your favourite stores for a copy.

We cannot discuss wealth creation without addressing the importance of knowledge, understanding, and wisdom. Let us check it out.

THE DIFFERENCE AND CONNECTION BETWEEN KNOWLEDGE, UNDERSTANDING AND WISDOM

When I was younger, I used to pray for wisdom, knowledge, and understanding. However, I later learned that I should have prayed for knowledge, understanding, and wisdom in that specific order as they naturally progress in that sequence. You cannot skip the first step and expect to reach the third effortlessly. It's akin to a child beginning their education in college instead of starting from preschool and gradually advancing. Just as a solid foundation is crucial for building a strong educational journey, starting with knowledge lays the groundwork for understanding, which then leads to wisdom.

Firstly, what is the meaning of knowledge, understanding, and wisdom?

> **Knowledge refers to the information and facts that a person has acquired through learning, experience, or education. It involves knowing about a particular subject, topic, or area of interest.**

Knowledge refers to the information and facts that a person has acquired through learning, experience, or education. It involves knowing about a particular subject, topic, or area of interest. Knowledge can be factual and is often based on data, evidence, or information that can be taught or learned. It represents what we know.

While a significant portion of knowledge comes from learning or experience, a percentage comes through instinct or spiritual means. As Pierre Teilhard de Chardin, the French philosopher, wisely stated, 'We are not human beings having a spiritual experience. We are spiritual beings having a human experience.' We possess an ability that transcends the physical realm, allowing us to know things without necessarily studying them. Hence, knowledge is considered one of the gifts of the spirit. This, however, does not negate the importance of studying and learning; instead, it emphasises the significance of harnessing both.

Take, for example, the story of Pharaoh in ancient Egypt. He gained knowledge of future events through a dream and not by reading about it. This highlights one way to acquire knowledge. Similarly, Daniel and his friends, despite their talent for interpreting dreams, had to undergo a three-year education at the University of Babylon. Their knowledge did not come without studying. This underscores the importance of reading and learning, as these provide the foundation for understanding and the wisdom necessary for achieving success, as we will soon see.

Now, what is understanding?

Understanding goes beyond mere knowledge. It involves comprehending, interpreting, and grasping the meaning or significance of information or knowledge. It's about making connections, seeing relationships, and being able to explain or apply what one knows. Understanding reflects how we process and make sense of knowledge.

For instance, consider Pharaoh's dream about the fat and thin cows. Pharaoh recounted the dream to his magicians while Joseph was in prison. **Pharaoh had knowledge of the dream but did not understand it.** Similarly, when he related it to them, his magicians acquired the knowledge of the dream, but they could not discern its meaning. This illustrates the distinction between knowledge and understanding.

When Joseph was summoned, the dream was narrated to him as well, but he possessed a gift that surpassed that of the magicians. He didn't just gain the knowledge of the dream; he understood it. Joseph could interpret the dream and extract its meaning, demonstrating what is referred to as understanding.

Have you ever read a book or passage without knowing its meaning or significance? We need to understand a subject to take full advantage of it. **Knowledge lacks utility without understanding.** The story of the biblical eunuch

> **Knowledge lacks utility without understanding.**

further illustrates this point, as he read the book of Isaiah but failed to understand it. When Philip asked if he comprehended what he read, the eunuch replied, *'How can I unless someone guides me?'*[19]

Now, Joseph could have simply interpreted the dreams and left. What do you think would have happened to the people without anyone providing the proper insight to prepare for the upcoming famine if he had not done that? This is where wisdom comes into play. Now, what is wisdom?

> **Wisdom is the capacity to make sound judgments, apply knowledge and understanding to real-life situations**

Wisdom is the capacity to make sound judgments, apply knowledge and understanding to real-life situations, and navigate complex challenges. Wisdom involves discernment, practical insight, and the ability to make informed and impactful decisions. **Put simply, wisdom is the application of knowledge and understanding.**

Joseph provided a solution to the foreseen challenge. He advised the creation of a reserve from the seven years of plenty, which would help them weather the storm of the impending famine. Joseph stressed that Pharaoh should appoint an administrator to oversee the food reserves during the years of abundance. Joseph's wisdom didn't stop at interpretation; it extended to practical action and leadership in implementing a plan that saved Egypt from disaster. **Wisdom provides solutions, and often, you are not compensated for your knowledge but for the solutions you offer.** Wisdom is the ultimate goal you should aspire. Imagine if Joseph had been clueless about the solution to the dream. Take a moment to imagine this. The purpose of knowledge and understanding is to provide a foundation for wisdom and, consequently, solutions and success.

He proposed a twenty per cent reserve, unlike the traditional tithe (ten per cent) he was accustomed to. **Wisdom does not always follow the path of common**

knowledge and tradition. I recently met a senior colleague who intrigued me with his understanding. He asked, "How curious are you about life?" He emphasised the importance of curiosity in achieving success. "You should be willing to question tradition and ask why things were done the way they were done. By seeking to understand why, you may discover insights others have overlooked." he continued. This is a practical way to engage your mind and explore the riches within it.

He shared an anecdote from his childhood when he unscrewed a lightbulb at less than ten years old and ventured into a well out of sheer curiosity. He acknowledged that pursuing curiosity might lead to taking a risky path, which could even be life-threatening. However, he stressed that it's essential not to remain ignorant.

> **Wisdom does not always follow the path of common knowledge and tradition.**

In conclusion, wisdom transcends mere knowledge or understanding; it represents the practical application of knowledge and understanding to achieve positive and far-reaching outcomes. Always consider what solutions you can proffer from what you know and understand. Remember that one can be a professor in a subject yet remain impoverished if they do not apply their knowledge.

5) SADLY, IT IS ONE OF THE MOST UNDERUTILISED RESOURCES

So far, we have uncovered four remarkable features of the mind. First, we acknowledge that the mind is a divine gift from God, freely given to help us fulfil our life's purpose. Next, we explored the mind's unparalleled creative power, recognising it as the driving force behind countless innovations and achievements. Thirdly, we examined the mind's dual nature, understanding that it holds both the power of life and death, capable of either transforming lives or causing destruction. Most recently, we delved into the mind's ability to create wealth, noting that it is the cornerstone of value creation and financial success.

As we continue our journey, we have come to the fifth intricate feature of the mind: **Sadly, it is one of the most underutilised resources.** Despite its immense potential and the profound impact it can have on our lives, the mind is often underutilised and undervalued. Many people fail to harness its full capabilities, missing out on opportunities for growth, innovation, and fulfilment. In this section, we will explore the reasons behind this neglect and how we can unlock the true potential of our minds.

> **They look for solutions outward, whereas the solution to their life problems is inward. Almost always, the answers to our prayers come in the form of ideas and concepts – this form of answered prayers is alien to many.**

i. Despite its immense potential, the mind remains one of the most underutilised resources. **Many people go through life**

without fully engaging their minds, often due to a lack of awareness or ignorance of the mind's capacity. They look for solutions outward, whereas the solution to their life problems is inward. Almost always, the answers to our prayers come in the form of ideas and concepts – this form of answered prayers is alien to many. This underutilisation is a significant loss, as the mind's capacity for creativity, problem-solving, and innovation is boundless. As Albert Einstein famously said, *"Imagination is more important than knowledge. For knowledge is limited, whereas imagination embraces the entire world, stimulating progress, giving birth to evolution."* This emphasises the power of your mind. Your mind has the power to dream, imagine, and create beyond your current realities, yet many do not take full advantage of this gift. In a way, you have a treasure that you need to mine.

ii. Apart from many people's ignorance of the mind's capacity, another reason for the underutilisation of this great resource is that they do not invest time in developing their mental capabilities. It takes time, dedication, and diligence to develop your mind. Though it involves dedication and discipline on your part, it is a worthy adventure as you will reap the rewards.

In a world filled with distractions, it's easy to neglect the discipline required to cultivate a powerful and focused mind. Regular activities like reading, meditation, and critical thinking exercises can significantly enhance our mental faculties, yet they are often overlooked in favour of more immediate gratifications.

iii. Additionally, the fear of failure or ridicule can prevent people from exploring their full potential and creativity. This fear can suppress creativity and innovation, causing individuals to settle for mediocrity instead of striving for greatness. As Sandy Gallagher rightly said, *"Everything you have ever desired is on the other side of fear"* Many times, what we fear isn't real. Therefore, I encourage you to be courageous and move beyond your fears to fulfil your potential. Have you been holding back on your journey to greatness because you fear what people will say about you? **Whether you start your journey or not, people will talk about you. Since they will, why not take the bold step to begin your journey and disregard their opinions?** Focus

> **Whether you start your journey or not, people will talk about you. Since they will, why not take the bold step to begin your journey and disregard their opinions?**

on getting better and moving closer to achieving your dreams each day. **You owe no one an explanation.**

This book aims to help you identify your greatest asset, which is your mind, and unlock its power for personal, financial, and professional success. **It is wrong and shortsighted to judge yourself by your present situation because there is so much potential within you that remains untapped.** Interestingly, you do not yet know the extent of what you can achieve, so I encourage you to step out of your comfort zone and discover your true potential. Exploring what you are capable of but have not yet attempted is an adventure you should be excited to embrace. It is an adventure of being introduced to yourself.

> **It is wrong and shortsighted to judge yourself by your present situation because there is so much potential within you that remains untapped.**

Many people leave their minds unattended and then wonder how they ended up where they are. The mind is like a field; if left uncared for, it will not remain bare but will grow weeds and thistles. The right approach is to cultivate the field and plant your desired seeds for the desired harvest. If you want to harvest success, you must recognise that your mind is your greatest asset and should not be neglected. Preparing the soil for the seed and nurturing the seedling to fruition takes effort. Focusing on the end result should encourage you to embrace such diligence.

The human mind has the capacity to conceive, create, and transform ideas into reality. The key to unlocking this potential lies in your willingness to invest in your mental capabilities, embrace your fears, and persistently pursue your dreams. As you cultivate your minds, you tap into a boundless source of creativity and innovation, setting the stage for success.

As we continue exploring the richest mine—the mind—let us commit to making the most of this extraordinary gift. The true wealth of the mind is not just in its capacity to dream but in its power to bring those dreams to life. Let us embark on this voyage with renewed determination, knowing that the mind, when fully engaged, holds the key to a future filled with limitless possibilities.

> **Many people leave their minds unattended and then wonder how they ended up where they are.**

As we conclude this chapter, it becomes evident that our thoughts, creativity, and capacity for wealth creation are intertwined with another crucial element of our lives: time. We have seen how the mind, a divine gift, holds the power to transform our world and shape our destinies. Now, we focus on the next chapter, 'The Gift of Time: Understanding its Value and Converting it into Success.' This is another precious gift given to us by the Creator, and it is important that we invest it wisely. In this new chapter, we will delve into the profound significance of time, an invaluable resource that, like the mind, can be harnessed to achieve extraordinary success. We will explore how to appreciate and utilise this precious gift effectively, ensuring that every moment contributes to our journey toward success and fulfilment. Let us embark on this new chapter with the understanding that harnessing time, much like our mind, is crucial to our success.

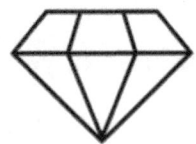

Chapter Two

The Gift of Time: Understanding Its Value and Converting It Into Success

"Time is free, but it's priceless. You can't own it, but you can use it. You can't keep it, but you can spend it. Once you've lost it, you can never get it back." — Harvey Mackay

In our journey through *"Exploring the Richest Mine: Harnessing the Power Within for Personal, Financial, and Professional Success,"* we have uncovered the incredible capabilities of the mind. It is time to turn our focus to another invaluable asset: time. Like the mind, time is a precious gift God gave you. It is a resource that cannot be bought or sold, yet it holds the potential to shape your lives in profound ways. If time could be bought, then some people would have lived thousands of years while others would barely afford a year, but interestingly, time cannot be bought or sold as we all have equal allocation irrespective of our gender, status, race or financial status.

> Though time is universal to us all, it determines who you are and who you will become.

Though time is universal to us all, it determines who you are and who you will become. The difference between each of us lies in how we use our time. Some people understand time and have found ways to harness it to their advantage, while others waste this precious gift. It's been said that some have found a way to buy time—meaning they have discovered how to pay to use their time for something more valuable rather than exchanging it for an extra dollar. We will explore this concept more closely in this chapter.

Consider two friends, Alex and Jordan, who are planning to attend an important business conference in a city 500 miles away. Alex decides to travel by bus because it's cheaper, while Jordan opts to fly even though it's more expensive.

> **The difference between each of us lies in how we use our time.**

Alex spends about $50 on the bus ticket, but the journey takes him ten hours. By the time he arrives, he's exhausted and has little time left to prepare for the conference. On the other hand, Jordan spends $200 on a plane ticket, but the flight only takes two hours. This means Jordan arrives well-rested and has an extra eight hours to prepare, network with other attendees, and strategies for the conference.

In this scenario, Jordan has effectively "bought time" by choosing the faster, albeit more expensive, mode of transportation. The additional time Jordan gained by flying allows him to focus on high-value activities contributing to his professional success, such as building connections and refining his presentation. Although he spent more money, the investment in time paid off through greater opportunities and a more impactful presence at the conference.

This example illustrates that sometimes, spending more money can be a strategic move to save time, enabling individuals to engage in activities that offer higher returns and lead to greater overall success.

Similarly, imagine a successful entrepreneur named Sarah who runs a thriving business. Early in her career, Sarah realised that she was spending countless hours on mundane tasks like scheduling appointments, responding to emails, and managing social media accounts. While these tasks were important, they did not directly contribute to the growth of her business or utilise her core strengths. Sarah understood that her time was her most valuable asset and decided to invest in hiring a virtual assistant. This decision allowed her to delegate these repetitive tasks and focus on strategic planning, product development, and networking — activities that would drive her business forward.

By "buying time" in this manner, Sarah was able to leverage her hours more effectively. "Buying time" in this context does not mean that she now has 26 hours in a day different from other people. Instead, it helped her save her allocated 24 hours to more profitable and valuable endeavours. The money she spent on the virtual assistant was a wise investment because it freed her up to engage in higher-value activities that generated significantly more revenue and growth for her business. As a result, Sarah not only saw a substantial increase in her company's success but also experienced a greater sense of fulfilment and balance in her life. This illustration also underscores the concept that, while we cannot create more time, we can choose to allocate our time towards activities that yield the highest returns, thereby maximising our potential for success.

One more example before we move on, consider the story of Juliet, a working mother of two. She understood the value of her time and made conscious decisions to maximise it. Instead of spending hours each week cleaning her home, she hired a cleaning service. The cost of the service was outweighed by the time she gained—time she could spend with her children, pursue her passion for writing, and even start a side business. Juliet's choice to delegate certain tasks allowed her to focus on activities that brought her joy and additional income, demonstrating how investing in time-saving services can lead to greater overall fulfilment and success.

These illustrations show how understanding the value of time and making strategic choices can lead to better outcomes. By investing in time-saving options, whether it's faster travel or outsourcing tasks, individuals can focus on more meaningful and productive activities, ultimately leading to greater success and satisfaction. I wrote a book titled **"From Overwhelmed to Organised: A time management blueprint for busy professionals."** You might want to check it out for some further details.

Time is unique in that it is equally distributed to everyone, regardless of wealth or status. Each of us is given 24 hours a day, no more, no less. How we choose to use this time determines the course of our lives. As Jim Rohn wisely said, *"Time is more valuable than money. You can get more money, but you cannot get more time."* This chapter aims to help you recognise the value of time, understand its significance, and learn how to convert it into tangible success.

The beauty of time lies in its flexibility. It can be saved and invested, and, unfortunately, it can also be wasted. Your current situation is a reflection of how you have managed your time thus far. Just as the

> **Every moment is a gift, and it is up to you to make the most of it.**

mind's potential can be harnessed for creativity and wealth, time can be strategically utilised to achieve personal, financial, and professional success. By understanding the true worth of time and making conscious decisions about how to spend it, you can unlock opportunities and pave the way for a fulfilling and prosperous life. As we explore the various facets of time and its impact on success, remember that **every moment is a gift, and it is up to you to make the most of it.**

TIME IS A FREE GIFT GIVEN TO US

Time is one of your most precious resources, yet it's often taken for granted. Unlike money or material possessions, time cannot be bought or borrowed; it is a gift freely given to you by your Creator. Everyone receives the same 24 hours a day, regardless of their wealth or status. This equal distribution underscores the intrinsic value of time and reminds you that every moment is a chance to make a difference in your life and the lives of others.

It is easy to overlook the significance of time amidst your daily myriads of activities. Understanding that time is a gift shifts your perspective to value its importance and appreciate the giver by utilising it appropriately. It encourages you to view each day as an opportunity to fulfil your purpose on earth. I could remember the story of Joshua, who was saddled with the responsibility of dividing the promised land among the children of Israel. He had all the resources to accomplish this purpose but could not because he was out of time. *"Now Joshua was old, advanced in years. And the LORD said to him: 'You are old, advanced in years, and there remains very much land yet to be possessed.'"*[20] This underscores the importance of time. **You do not have all the time in the world to engage in every activity that comes your way.** It is a precious resource but limited, and the onus is on you to manage it both effectively and efficiently. As the saying goes, *"Time is the most valuable thing a man can spend."*

> **You do not have all the time in the world to engage in every activity that comes your way.**

There is a difference between managing something effectively and efficiently. Understanding this concept will help you align yourself on the path to success.

Managing Time Effectively And Efficiently

The terms "effectiveness" and "efficiency" are often mistakenly used interchangeably, but they hold distinct meanings. Effectiveness is a concept that measures how well **tasks are performed to achieve desired outcomes,** reflecting the success in meeting targeted goals. On the other hand, **efficiency refers to executing tasks with minimal time and resource wastage, ensuring that work is completed quickly and accurately.** Efficiency minimises work input for a desired output, reducing wastage, while effectiveness is about driving to the right result. **So, one can do the wrong thing efficiently.**

> So, one can do the wrong thing efficiently.

These concepts are frequently applied in management to evaluate performance. Understanding the difference between effectiveness and efficiency is crucial for assessing and improving productivity. Now, let's explore the key distinctions between these two terms.

Definition, Focus, and Orientation

1. Effectiveness refers to the extent to which someone or something achieves the desired outcome or goal. It measures how well objectives are met, while efficiency involves performing tasks with minimal wastage of time and resources, ensuring work is completed swiftly and accurately.
2. Effectiveness concentrates on the accuracy and success of the task in meeting its goals, while Efficiency Focuses on the process, ensuring tasks are done correctly with optimal use of resources and minimal time.
3. Effectiveness is strategy-oriented, aiming at achieving the desired end result, while

efficiency is operation-oriented, concerned with a task's inputs and outputs.

4. Effectiveness is not necessarily effort-oriented; it's more about the outcome rather than the effort put in. Efficiency is effort-oriented; it emphasises reducing effort and resources while achieving the desired outcome.

5. Effectiveness is not specifically time-oriented; its primary concern is whether the end goals are met. While efficiency is time-oriented, it focuses on completing tasks in the shortest possible time with the least waste.

Bringing this concept into time management, effectively managing time means focusing on doing the right things that align with your goals and values. It involves prioritising tasks and activities that contribute to your long-term objectives and vision. In simple terms, effectively managing time is about doing the right things with your time rather than just keeping busy. **Remember, not all good things are right for**

you—engaging in something that seems good may not necessarily be the right thing for you to do.

Imagine you're a busy professional with a clear goal of advancing in your career. You're working hard to complete a key project that will significantly contribute to your long-term objectives. One day, you receive an invitation to join a local book club, which seems like a great opportunity to network and engage with others. While the book club is a positive and enriching activity, it may not align with your immediate goal of finishing your project. Attending the book club might divert valuable time and focus away from your current project. Even though the book club is good in this scenario, it's not the right fit for your current priorities. By focusing on your project and postponing joining the book club for a later date, you ensure that you're investing your time in ways that

> Remember, not all good things are right for you—engaging in something that seems good may not necessarily be the right thing for you to do.

truly advance your current and long-term goals. It is important to know that you are not meant to do all good things but the good thing that is right for you. In so doing, you effectively manage your time, which is a priceless and scarce resource.

To further reiterate that not all good things are right for you, let us consider the story of Jesus visiting the home of Mary and Martha, as depicted in the Bible. Martha busied herself with preparations and serving, ensuring everything was perfect for their guest. Her intentions were good—she wanted to provide a welcoming environment and honour Jesus with her hospitality. Meanwhile, Mary chose to sit at Jesus' feet to listen to His teachings.

When Martha became frustrated and asked Jesus to tell Mary to help her, Jesus responded that Mary had chosen the better part. Despite Martha's good intentions, her focus on the immediate tasks of serving and preparing, though commendable, was not the best choice at that moment. Mary's decision to prioritise learning and engagement with Jesus was more aligned with the significance of the visit. This illustrates that even when activities seem good and valuable, they may not always align with the most important priorities at the time. Prioritising what truly matters in a given context ensures that your efforts are directed toward the most meaningful outcomes, which is the concept of managing your time effectively.

Being effective ensures that your time leads us towards your desired outcomes. It's about ensuring that your actions significantly impact and bring you closer to fulfilling your purpose. For instance, spending time on personal development, building relationships, and working on meaningful projects are all examples of effective time management. I wrote a book titled **"From Overwhelmed to Organised: A time management blueprint for busy professionals."** You might want to check it out for some further details.

On the other hand, efficiency is about doing things correctly with minimal waste of time and resources. It involves finding the quickest and most streamlined methods to complete tasks. Efficiency is crucial for maximising productivity and ensuring you make the best use of your limited time. For example, using technology to automate repetitive tasks, delegating responsibilities, and minimising distractions are ways to manage time efficiently. While efficiency is about the process, effectiveness is about the outcome.

> **Being efficient without being effective can lead to doing a lot of work that doesn't necessarily bring you closer to your goals. Conversely, being effective but not efficient can result in slow progress and wasted time.**

The lesson is that you should both be effective and efficient in managing your time. **Being efficient without being effective can lead to doing a lot of work that doesn't necessarily bring you closer to your**

goals. Conversely, being effective but not efficient can result in slow progress and wasted time. To truly honour the gift of time, you must strive to be both effective and efficient. This means setting clear priorities, focusing on meaningful activities, and optimising your processes to achieve your goals with the least amount of time and effort.

Imagine setting out on a journey to a destination south but taking a flight north. Although flying is an efficient mode of travel, this approach is ineffective because it moves you farther from your destination. Similarly, if you were to travel south but instead of going by air, you journeyed by bicycle, taking the right direction to your destination — the slow pace would compromise your efficiency, though you are heading in the right direction. This illustrates the importance of aligning effectiveness with efficiency. Being efficient without being effective is like speeding in the wrong direction while being effective but inefficient can result in prolonged and wasted time. So, as you journey in life, embrace effectiveness and efficiency in managing your time, and you will definitely end up successful.

To truly harness the power of time, you must ensure that your actions are both effective and efficient. This means not only choosing the right tasks that bring you closer to your goals but also performing those tasks in the most streamlined and productive manner possible. By integrating effectiveness with efficiency, you avoid the pitfalls of wasted effort and misdirected energy, ultimately making the best use of your precious gift of time. Embracing both principles allows you to navigate your journey towards success with clarity and purpose, ensuring that each moment spent is a step closer to achieving your aspirations.

A Structured Approach To Managing Your Time Effectively And Efficiently

To effectively and efficiently manage your time, it's crucial to have a structured approach. This is where the Time Management Matrix, often associated with Stephen Covey's time management principles, comes into play. This powerful tool helps you categorise and prioritise your tasks based on their urgency and importance. By understanding where your activities fall within this matrix, you can make more informed decisions about where to focus your efforts, ensuring that you are working hard and smart. This section will delve into the Time Management Matrix, exploring how it can guide you in aligning your actions with your goals, thus enhancing your effectiveness and efficiency.

The Matrix, also known as the Eisenhower Matrix, is a powerful tool for organising tasks and prioritising time effectively. It divides tasks into four distinct categories based on urgency and importance. This matrix helps you make informed decisions about allocating your time, ensuring you focus on what truly matters.

Quadrant I: Urgent and Important

Tasks in this quadrant require immediate attention and have significant consequences. These are often crises, deadlines, or problems that need urgent resolution. Handling these tasks effectively prevents them from escalating further.

Quadrant II: Not Urgent but Important

Tasks in this category are crucial for long-term success and personal growth but do not require immediate action. These include strategic planning, relationship building, and personal development. Prioritising these activities helps prevent them from becoming urgent and ensures continuous progress toward your vision and goals.

Quadrant III: Urgent but Not Important

Tasks in this quadrant demand immediate attention but do not significantly contribute to your long-term goals. They often involve interruptions or distractions that can be delegated or minimised. Managing these tasks efficiently involves finding ways to reduce their impact on valuable time.

Quadrant IV: Not Urgent and Not Important

Tasks in this quadrant are neither urgent nor important and often involve time-wasting activities or trivial matters. Eliminating these tasks frees up time for more meaningful and productive activities.

By utilising this Time Management Matrix, you can categorise your tasks and focus on what matters most, ensuring both effective and efficient use of your time.

Examples of tasks in each quadrant of the time management matrix

Quadrant I: Urgent and Important

1. **Emergency Medical Situations:** Addressing a sudden health crisis that requires immediate medical attention.
2. **Critical Work Deadlines:** Completing a project or report due today that impacts key business operations.
3. **Resolving a Major Customer Complaint:** Fixing a significant issue that affects a major

client that could harm the company's reputation if not addressed immediately.
4. **Household Emergencies:** Dealing with a burst pipe or electrical problem that requires urgent repair to prevent damage.

Quadrant II: Not Urgent but Important
1. **Strategic Planning:** Developing a long-term business strategy or personal growth plan to shape your future.
2. **Building Relationships:** Nurturing personal or professional relationships through regular communication and engagement.
3. **Exercise and Health:** Committing to a regular workout routine or health check-ups to ensure well-being.
4. **Skill Development:** Learning a new skill or taking a course that will enhance career prospects or personal growth.

5. **Personal Goals:** Setting and working towards personal goals, such as writing a book or learning a new language.

Quadrant III: Urgent but Not Important

1. **Interruptions by Colleagues:** Responding to frequent, non-critical interruptions from colleagues that disrupt your workflow.
2. **Low-priority Emails:** Addressing emails that need a quick response but do not significantly impact your overall objectives.
3. **Meeting Invitations:** Attending meetings that are scheduled urgently but do not contribute significantly to your core responsibilities.
4. **Unplanned Calls:** Handling phone calls or messages that require immediate attention but do not affect your important tasks.
5. **Routine Administrative Tasks:** Completing minor administrative work that feels urgent but does not align with your major goals.

Quadrant IV: Not Urgent and Not Important

1. **Social Media Browsing:** Spending time scrolling through social media without any specific purpose.
2. **Excessive Television Watching:** Watching TV shows or movies that do not contribute to your personal or professional development.
3. **Unnecessary Online Shopping:** Engaging in online shopping or browsing for items that are not needed and do not provide immediate value.
4. **Gossiping:** Participating in conversations or activities that do not add value to your personal or professional life.

These examples above should clarify how different tasks fit into each quadrant of the Time Management Matrix.

Overview of the Time Management Matrix with examples

	URGENT	NOT URGENT
IMPORTANT	**Quadrant I** 1. Emergency Medical Situations 2. Critical Work Deadlines 3. Resolving a Major Customer Complaint 4. Household Emergencies	**Quadrant II** 1. Strategic Planning 2. Building Relationships 3. Exercise and Health 4. Skill Development 5. Personal Goals
NOT IMPORTANT	**Quadrant III** 1. Interruptions by Colleagues 2. Low-priority Emails 3. Meeting Invitations 4. Unplanned Calls 5. Routine Administrative Tasks	**Quadrant IV** 1. Social Media Browsing 2. Excessive Television Watching 3. Unnecessary Online Shopping 4. Gossiping

Now that you have assigned a task to its quadrant, what is next?

Once you have assigned tasks to their respective quadrants in the Time Management Matrix, the next step is to determine what actions to take for each category. This approach will help you manage your time effectively and efficiently, maximising productivity and minimising stress.

For tasks in Quadrant I, which are both urgent and important, immediate attention is required. These tasks often represent crises or pressing problems that you can't ignore without severe consequences. Addressing these tasks promptly is crucial because neglecting them can come with great consequences. Prioritise these tasks first, ensuring you allocate adequate time and resources to resolve them swiftly and effectively.

In Quadrant II, you'll find important but not urgent tasks. These activities, such as strategic planning, personal development, and building relationships, are key to your long-term success. While they may not demand immediate attention, neglecting them can lead to a buildup of Quadrant I crises. It's essential to schedule regular time blocks for these tasks to foster growth, prevent future emergencies, and ensure continuous improvement. Investing time here can significantly and positively impact your life in the long run.

For tasks in Quadrant III, which are urgent but not important, it's essential to recognise that while they demand your attention, they may not contribute significantly to your long-term goals. Often, you can delegate these tasks to others, freeing up your time for more impactful activities. By identifying and delegating Quadrant III tasks, you can focus on your higher-priority tasks without getting sidetracked by less important matters.

Quadrant IV tasks, which are neither urgent nor important, should be minimised or eliminated. These activities are often time-wasters that do not contribute to your productivity or goals. Recognising and cutting down on Quadrant IV tasks allows you to reclaim valuable time that can be better spent on more meaningful activities. This involves being honest with yourself about your habits and consciously eliminating distractions and non-productive activities from your routine.

Now that you have learned how to handle your daily tasks, it is time to act on what you have learnt, and in so doing, you will put yourself on the path to success.

CAN TIME BE BOUGHT?

"**In Time,**" a 2011 movie directed by Andrew Niccol, portrays time as a universal currency. In the movie, people stop ageing at 25. They have to earn, buy, or steal time to stay alive. The wealthy can live forever, while the poor struggle to gain enough time to see the next day. As much as this sounds interesting, can time be bought?

Even if you had a thousand years to yourself, as portrayed in the movie, you couldn't have more than twenty-four hours a day, which shows that, in the real sense, you cannot buy

> **Time is more important than money.**

time. Time is a priceless gift given to everyone equally per day, irrespective of their status. As long as an individual is alive, he has 24 hours per day, just like every other person. No amount of money can truly buy time. This underscores the value of time and the necessity to use it wisely. Just as the characters in "In Time" faced the dire consequences of running out of time, you must acknowledge that you can run out of time – everyone will definitely run out of time one day.

Interestingly, you can buy or acquire more money, but you cannot do the same with time. This highlights that **time is more important than money.** Some people say that time is money because you can convert time to money, but in reality, time is more valuable and transcends money in value. Thus, time is not money. While money can provide comfort, it cannot extend the hours of your day. Therefore, it is crucial to understand the true value of time and prioritise how you spend it.

You have seen that time cannot be bought; once a moment passes, it is gone forever. If time cannot be purchased, the question then becomes: *what can we do with it, or how can we get more of it?* The answer lies in your ability to manage time; saving time effectively is an important way to acquire more time. Time-saving strategies involve making deliberate choices about how you allocate your hours, ensuring that you use them in ways that align with your priorities and goals. By becoming more efficient and organised, you can maximise the productivity of your time, essentially "saving" it for the activities that matter most.

One way to save time is through careful planning and prioritisation. As Benjamin Franklin wisely said, *"By failing to prepare, you are preparing to fail."* Creating and sticking to a structured schedule prevents you from wasting precious minutes on unnecessary tasks or distractions. You are more likely to save time and be productive if you write down your plan for the day before you step out in the morning. You should write out the plan before going to bed the previous day, as this helps condition your mind to get the job done.

This is just one of the ways to save time. While you cannot buy more time, you can certainly learn to save and invest it wisely, leading to a more successful and fulfilling life.

Let us use this illustration to demonstrate saving time, which might resonate with you. Meanwhile, I can relate to how one can be overwhelmed with tasks as a busy professional, and I have found practical ways to go round this to achieve both personal and professional success. I have packaged this in a book, "From Overwhelmed to Organised: A time management blueprint for busy professionals." You may want to check it out, so let us go back to our illustration.

Imagine Jane, a working professional with a busy schedule that includes her job, family responsibilities, and personal goals. Jane starts her day by planning out her tasks using a sticky note to save time. She prioritises these tasks, setting specific blocks of time for each task based on their urgency and importance, utilising the time management matrix. Instead of checking her email constantly, she designates two specific times in the day to manage her inbox, which prevents interruptions and allows her to focus better on her tasks. She also took advantage of an email do-not-distract feature to reduce distractions and a social media blocker feature to stay focused on her most important tasks for the day.

Jane also identifies tasks that can be delegated or outsourced. She hires a cleaning service to handle household chores, freeing up her weekends to spend quality time with her family and pursue her hobbies. Additionally, she uses meal planning and batch cooking on Sundays after church service, which reduces the daily stress of deciding what to cook and saves her time during the week. By implementing these strategies, Jane effectively saves time, which she then invests in activities that contribute to her personal and professional growth, leading to a more productive, organised and balanced life. Can you implement a similar strategy to save time and invest in more productive endeavours?

SAVING AND INVESTING TIME FOR SUCCESS

We often talk about how we use time by saying we "spend" it. You would have heard someone say, "I spent time studying, or I spent time seeing a movie." This word 'spend' is significant because it highlights that time, much like money, is a currency that we spend. We all possess an equal amount of this currency each day. Everyone receives the same 24 hours, regardless of their status or circumstances. The critical question, then, is how do you spend your time? **Just as your financial decisions determine your wealth, your time management decisions determine your success.** The difference between the rich and the poor, the successful and the unsuccessful, often lies in how they spend their time, and this is our focus in this section- time can be saved and invested for success.

In the same way that careful budgeting and wise investments can grow your financial wealth, saving and investing your time effectively and efficiently can lead to personal and professional growth and success. The wealthy and successful often have a more deliberate approach to spending their time. They prioritise activities that yield the highest returns, whether it's learning new skills, building relationships, or working on projects that align with their goals. By contrast, those who struggle often find their time consumed by low-value tasks or distractions, leaving little room for growth. You may want to check the section *"A Structured Approach to Managing Your Time Effectively and Efficiently"* on how to manage your time more effectively and efficiently. In doing so, you align yourself for great success.

Understanding time as a currency helps you see the importance of saving and investing it wisely. Saving time means finding ways to be more efficient and cutting out unnecessary activities. Investing time involves putting effort into activities that will pay off in the long run. By being intentional about how you spend your time, you can make the most of this invaluable resource and pave the way for greater success in all areas of your life.

It is ironic how much effort many put into protecting their money compared to how little thought they give to safeguarding their time. They go to great lengths to create safety measures for their money, like safety boxes, wallets, and bank accounts, all designed to keep their money secure. Yet, when it comes to their time, a far more valuable and finite currency, they spend it without much consideration. They carefully track every penny they spend but let hours slip away unaccounted for, often wasted on activities that do not contribute to their growth or happiness.

How do you feel when you misplace or lose your money? Have you ever felt bad about losing time?

Have you ever even considered that you lost or wasted time before? Take a moment to think about these questions.

Imagine if you have a thousand dollars in your wallet, and I walked up to you and asked you to hand over the wallet. Would you give it to me just like that? Wouldn't you ask questions? This is because you do not want to lose your money. Now, imagine if I walked up to you and started chatting or gossiping with you or visited you unannounced with a video game. Would your reaction be the same as when I asked you for your wallet? Would you just go ahead and allow me to spend your time chatting or playing a video game with you? This highlights how much importance you place on our time, and this illustration could come in different shades.

Imagine if you treated your time with the same reverence you give to your money. What if you had "time wallets" or "time accounts" where you consciously deposited and withdrew your hours? The irony is that the same people who are meticulous about not letting a single dollar go out without consideration often let their time, which is irreplaceable, be squandered on trivial pursuits. Unlike money, time cannot be earned back once it is spent. This makes it even more crucial to protect and invest your time wisely.

More than safeguarding your money, you should be vigilant in managing your time because it is priceless. Time is a finite resource that, once lost, can never be regained. Each moment holds the potential for value creation, personal growth, and meaningful experiences. By being mindful of how you spend your time, you can ensure that you make the most of your days and propel yourself toward your goals. This shift in perspective can transform not only how you view time but also how you live your life, making every moment count.

Before heading to the grocery store, you probably prepare a list of items you want to buy. This list ensures that you spend your money wisely and efficiently, avoiding unnecessary purchases and saving money during your shopping trip. Do you take the same approach regarding your daily allocation of 24 hours? **Do you create a "grocery list" for your time, planning out how you will spend each hour, or do you simply show up at the "supermarket of the day" and allow yourself to spend your time on every activity that comes your way?**

> **Do you create a "grocery list" for your time, planning out how you will spend each hour, or do you simply show up at the "supermarket of the day" and allow yourself to spend your time on every activity that comes your way?**

Consider how different your day could be if you approached it with the same level of planning and intention as a trip to the grocery store. Without a plan, it's easy to drift through the day, embracing whatever demands your time or whatever distractions arise - ending up feeling like you haven't accomplished anything meaningful. But with a clear list of priorities and tasks, you can navigate your day with purpose, making deliberate choices about how to spend your time in activities that align with your goals and values.

Having a "grocery list" for your time helps you stay focused and ensures that you spend your hours on what truly matters. It allows you to avoid wasting time on low-value activities and enables you to make the most of each moment. By planning your day, you can allocate specific blocks of time to important tasks, set aside moments for relaxation and self-care, and create a balanced schedule that promotes both productivity and well-being. Just as you wouldn't go to the supermarket without a list, don't navigate your day without a plan. Treat your time as the precious, finite resource it is, and spend it wisely to create the successful life you deserve.

It is no longer news that you should appreciate the gift of time God gave you by saving and investing it. Let's take this a step further.

Do you know that saving and investing are different? If you cut down on your budget each month and manage to put together a thousand dollars after three months - that is an example of saving your money. You might place this money in a savings account at a bank, which is a way of safeguarding your funds. But what if you took that same money and put it in a fixed deposit or used it to buy shares in the same bank? Even though you are interacting with the same bank, you are engaging at different levels—one at the level of savings and the other at the level of investing. This clearly shows that saving is different from investing.

The same principle applies to time. You can save and/or invest time. Imagine you manage to streamline your daily tasks, freeing up an extra hour each day. That's saving time. However, if you take that saved hour and use it to learn a new skill, start a side project, or build relationships, you are investing your time. While saving time is about efficiency, investing time is about effectiveness and growth. It is preferable to both save and invest your time for greater returns. By doing so, you make the most of every moment and ensure that your efforts today lead to a more prosperous and fulfilling tomorrow.

Imagine you had the option to watch a Premier League football match this weekend, an exciting experience that would consume approximately two hours of your time. Instead of watching the full match, you chose to only watch the 5-minute highlights after the game. This decision saves you more than an hour and a half of your time. By saving that time, you free up a portion of your day, which you then decide to invest in something more valuable.

For instance, you can use the time you save to take a Udemy course on mastering Excel or improving your communication skills. This course, which also lasts for about the same amount of time you saved, becomes a productive investment of your time. While watching the full match might offer immediate excitement and entertainment, spending the saved time on learning a new skill contributes to your long-term success and personal growth. This strategic approach to saving and investing time illustrates how you can prioritise activities that align with your goals and aspirations.

In everyday life, such decisions are crucial. Opting for highlights over full matches is just one example of how you can manage your time more efficiently. By consistently making choices that save time and then investing it in activities that propel you towards your purpose in life, you edge closer to achieving a more fulfilling and successful life. Remember, it's not just about saving time but investing it wisely to build a brighter future.

Remember: Time Can Be Wasted

In our journey through understanding and converting the gift of time for success, we've explored the significance of saving and investing time. Just as you can save and invest time to achieve your goals, you must also be aware that time can be wasted. Recognising the potential for time wastage is crucial to maintaining a balanced and effective approach to engaging time.

While saving and investing time leads to productivity and growth, wasting time can result in missed opportunities and unfulfilled potential. It's essential for you to be mindful of how you allocate your time, ensuring that you don't fall into the trap of spending your precious hours on activities that do not contribute to your goals. In this section, we'll delve into the various ways time can be wasted and how to avoid these pitfalls so you can make the most of every moment.

> **One of the most common ways time is wasted is through procrastination.**

One of the most common ways time is wasted is through procrastination. When you delay tasks or put off important activities, you lose valuable time and add unnecessary stress to your life. Procrastination often leads to last-minute rushes and subpar work, which can hinder your progress and productivity. Overcoming procrastination involves setting clear goals, breaking tasks into smaller, manageable steps, and maintaining a disciplined schedule. Self-discipline is key to overcoming procrastination. Instead of making excuses to embark on the task, just jump on it and get it done.

> Another significant time-waster is engaging in unproductive activities, such as excessive social media use, binge-watching television shows, or mindlessly browsing the internet.

Another significant time-waster is engaging in unproductive activities, such as excessive social media use, binge-watching television shows, or

mindlessly browsing the internet. While these activities can be enjoyable, they often consume more time than intended and offer little to no value in terms of personal or professional growth. It's important to set boundaries and limit these distractions to ensure that your time is spent on activities that align with your goals and aspirations.

I am almost sure that I am not the only one who, while reading, for instance, and wanting to look up the meaning of a word on my phone, found myself spending 5 minutes, then 10 minutes, and eventually 30 minutes checking notifications. These could be emails, social media updates, or breaking news alerts. I realised this was distracting me from meaningful tasks and causing unnecessary time wastage. To combat this, I set specific times for checking notifications and put my phone on focused mode during work sessions. Can you relate to this? What strategies have you implemented to avoid distractions and invest your time more wisely? Taking these steps can help you stay on track and achieve tremendous success.

Poor planning and lack of prioritisation can also lead to wasted time. Without a clear plan or a prioritised list of tasks, you may find yourself jumping from one activity to another without making meaningful progress. This can create **a sense of busyness without actual productivity**. By organising your tasks, setting priorities, and creating a structured plan, you can ensure that your time is used effectively and that you are consistently moving towards your objectives.

Consider this scenario: If I asked you to help with a task, you might say you're busy, which is understandable. But what if I mentioned that helping with the task comes with a cash prize of ten thousand dollars? Would you still maintain that you are too busy to take up the task? When I presented this to a group, everyone burst into laughter because they realised that being busy is really about priority. The moment I attached a cash prize, the task I requested shot up their priority list. They were ready to sacrifice other activities for the new one because of the monetary reward.

This example underscores an important point: What you claim to be busy with reflects your priorities. When you say you're busy, are the tasks you're engaged in truly worth your time, or are you merely whiling away the hours? It's crucial to evaluate the activities that consume your day. Are they helping you achieve your goals or just distractions that keep you from making meaningful progress? Time is a precious resource, and how you choose to spend it determines the trajectory of your life.

To avoid the pitfalls of wasting time, as mentioned earlier, the first step is to cultivate awareness of how you spend your time. Track your daily activities for a week to identify patterns and pinpoint where your time goes. This self-assessment can reveal surprising habits and distractions that you may not have noticed. With this information, you can make conscious decisions to eliminate or reduce activities that do not contribute to your goals or well-being. For instance, setting specific times for checking emails and social media can prevent these activities from eating into your productive hours.

> **Cultivate an awareness of how you spend your time.**

Another effective strategy is to set clear, achievable goals and break them down into manageable tasks. When you have a clear vision of what you want to accomplish, it becomes easier to prioritise your tasks and focus on what truly matters. Use tools like to-do lists, planners, or digital apps to organise your tasks and set deadlines. By planning your day ahead, you can allocate your time more efficiently and ensure that you are progressing toward your goals.

> **Set clear, achievable goals and break them down into manageable tasks.**

Remember to include time for breaks and self-care to maintain your energy and motivation through out the day.

Lastly, learn to say no to activities and commitments that do not align with your priorities. It is easy to get overwhelmed by taking on too many responsibilities or agreeing to activities that do not add value to your life. By setting boundaries and being selective about where you invest your time, you can protect your time for what truly matters. As the saying goes, "Time is what we want most, but what we use worst." - William Penn.

By making intentional choices about how you spend your time, you can avoid wasting it and instead use it to create a fulfilling and successful life.

Your Success Reflects Your Time Management

In the previous section, we explored the various ways time can be wasted and the impact of such wastage on your journey toward success. It's clear that how you spend your time significantly influences the outcomes you achieve. This leads us to a crucial realisation: your success is a direct reflection of how you manage your time. **You are a product of how you have managed your time.**

Consider this quote by Jim Rohn: "Time is more valuable than money. You can get more money, but you cannot get more time." This underscores the importance of time management in achieving your goals and dreams. You

> **You are a product of how you have managed your time.**

lay the groundwork for personal, financial, and professional success by managing your time effectively. In this section, we will consider how your time management practices shape your future, emphasising that how you allocate and prioritise your time is instrumental in determining your level of success.

You might often blame others for your failures, seeking external reasons to explain your predicament. It's often easier to point fingers outward rather than look inward. However, the truth is that you are usually the reason for where you are. Your success is determined by how you have spent your time.

To be objective with yourself, take a notepad and a pen and write down what you engage in throughout the day. List your activities and, if possible, use a time tracker app to see how much time you spend on various tasks. Repeat this exercise for one week. This will give you an overview of how you spend your time.

Next, go through the activities one by one and ask yourself, "Does this task move me toward success?" Tick "yes" or "no" beside each activity. Once you are done, look at your total hours on high-impact versus low-impact activities. Then ask yourself, "If I continue this way for 5 years, would I end up successful or a failure?" This exercise will reveal whether your current habits genuinely reflect the level of success you have achieved or aspire to achieve.

By analysing your daily activities and time expenditures, you can identify patterns and areas for improvement. It becomes evident that success doesn't just happen by chance; it is cultivated through conscious and deliberate time management.

ADOPT A SENSE OF URGENCY REGARDING YOUR ACTIVITIES.

To truly get the best from every time you have gotten, it's crucial to adopt a sense of urgency regarding your activities. The concept of urgency isn't about rushing; it's about recognising that your time is limited and must be used wisely. As articulated by the Great Teacher, "I must work the works of Him who sent Me while it is day; the night is coming when no one can work."[21] This profound insight underscores the necessity of acting with intention and purpose now rather than postponing tasks. The finite nature of time means that if you want to achieve your goals and experience success, you must engage in activities that advance you towards those goals without delay. Why? Because you might not have the time to implement your ideas even if you are willing to do so if you run out of time.

Another translation of this verse captures the essence even more clearly: *"We must quickly carry out the tasks assigned us by the one who sent us. The night is coming, and then no one can work."* NLT This emphasises the urgency of acting swiftly and decisively. Just as day turns to night, presenting a period when work is no longer possible, the same principle applies to your life and career. Time is said to wait for no one. Remember that money lost can be regained, but not time.

Consider this: the tasks you prioritise and how you use your time directly reflect your commitment to success. When you approach each day with a clear sense of urgency and purpose, you align your actions with your goals, creating a direct pathway to achieving them. This focus maximises your productivity and ensures that each moment spent is a step towards success rather than drifting aimlessly.

A good example of the critical nature of time management is found in the story of Joshua. Despite having been granted every resource necessary for success, Joshua faced a sobering reality as he grew older. The Bible recounts in Joshua 13:1 (NLT), *"When Joshua was an old man, the LORD said to him, 'You are growing old, and much land remains to be conquered.'"* Despite being given a clear purpose and the means to fulfil it, Joshua was confronted with the stark realisation that time had slipped away, leaving him with unfinished tasks. This serves as a powerful reminder of the importance of managing our time wisely and with urgency. Just as Joshua did, you do not want to run out of time.

Joshua's situation illustrates that even with the best resources and intentions, time remains finite. The goals and purposes you set for yourself require not just planning and resources but also timely action. If you allow yourself to be complacent or waste your time on trivial pursuits, you risk finding yourself in a position where you are too late to accomplish what you once set out to do. This underscores the urgency with which you should approach your own goals. You have the advantage of youth and energy, and it is crucial to channel these resources into meaningful work that propels you towards your aspirations.

> **Your time is a precious asset that will not last forever.**

Consider this: **your time is a precious asset that will not last forever.** Just as Joshua was reminded of his unfinished tasks when it was too late to accomplish them entirely, you must be vigilant about how you allocate your time too. Reflect on your daily activities and assess whether they align with your long-term goals. Are you investing your time in high-impact tasks that will drive you toward success, or are you allowing it to slip away on less significant endeavours? Remember, you are a product of how you have managed your time. Embrace this urgency and make every moment count towards achieving your true potential.

TIME ONCE LOST CANNOT BE REGAINED: THE IMPACT OF PERSONAL CHOICES ON YOUR LIFESPAN AND POTENTIAL.

Time is an irreplaceable resource; once it's gone, it cannot be regained. Unlike money, which can be lost and then regained—sometimes even multiplied—time, once spent, is permanently gone. For example, if you squander two hours of your day on trivial activities or distractions, those two hours are lost forever. You cannot add them to your 24-hour allotment for the day; you can only focus on making the most of the remaining hours.

However, a more profound and often overlooked aspect of time management is the effect of personal choices on your lifespan and overall potential. When individuals engage in harmful behaviours, such as excessive smoking or drinking, they don't merely lose time due to the direct consequences of these actions but also potentially shorten their lifespan. For instance, if someone is destined to live for 90 years but, due to reckless lifestyle choices, only lives to 60, they have effectively lost 30 years of potential time. Those lost years could have been filled with opportunities for growth, achievement, and fulfilment.

Even if the individual manages to live the entire 90 years, the quality of those years may be compromised. A life lived in poor health often results in reduced energy levels, diminished productivity, and lower overall effectiveness in achieving goals. Thus, time lost due to poor health choices affects not only the quantity of life but also its quality.

Maintaining a healthy lifestyle ensures that you can fully utilise your time for productive and meaningful activities. Your health is a key component to reaching your full potential. Thus, safeguarding your health is not just about extending your life but also about ensuring that you can make the most of every moment you have.

As we recognise the importance of personal choices in managing our time and health, it's equally crucial to acknowledge that systemic factors also play a significant role in how time is valued and utilised. In some parts of the world, policies, inadequate healthcare systems, poverty, and conflict can dramatically impact an individual's lifespan and potential. For instance, consider a woman who could have lived an additional 50 years. Her life might be cut short due to preventable delivery-associated complications, exacerbated by a lack of access to proper medical care or education. Similarly, children born into poverty or conflict zones may suffer from malnutrition and inadequate healthcare, drastically reducing their chances of reaching their full potential.

These systemic issues highlight a sobering reality: time and life can be lost not just due to personal choices but also because of societal and structural failures. The examples of individuals affected by poor healthcare systems or socio-economic conditions are numerous and heart-wrenching. They serve as a reminder of the critical need for systemic changes that prioritise health, long life and well-being. This is not only a moral obligation but also a fundamental human right. Every individual deserves the opportunity to live a full and productive life, free from the constraints imposed by inadequate infrastructure or political instability.

This situation calls for a collective effort from individuals, leaders, and nations to address these systemic issues. By improving healthcare systems, combating poverty, and fostering peace, we can help ensure that more people have the opportunity to live out their full potential. It's essential for those in positions of power to implement policies that protect and enhance the quality of life for all. For individuals, it's a call to advocate for and support systemic changes that give everyone a fair chance at achieving their goals and dreams. The collective action towards these improvements will ultimately benefit not only the individuals directly affected but also society as a whole by fostering a more equitable and thriving global community.

THE OVERLOOKED TREASURE

Having explored how time, once lost, cannot be regained and the impact of personal choices on lifespan and potential, it is vital to delve into another crucial aspect: the overlooked treasure. Despite its undeniable significance, time is often overlooked and not given the appropriate attention it deserves. While money, possessions, and other tangible assets are commonly protected and cherished, time, which is far more precious, is frequently taken for granted.

Consider the words of the ancient philosopher Seneca: *"It is not that we have a short time to live, but that we waste a lot of it."* This quote underscores a fundamental truth—time is a valuable resource, yet it is often squandered on activities that do not contribute to our goals or well-being. Unlike money, which can be regained, time flows in one direction. Once a moment passes, it is gone forever, making it imperative to use it wisely.

Just as we have seen earlier about the mind being a powerful tool but usually underutilised, time, likewise, which is a precious gift, is often overlooked and not given the regard due to it. Imagine if everyone turned each minute into something meaningful and productive—what would the world look like? It is, however, quite unfortunate that many do not even know the value of their time, let alone think of saving and investing it to achieve success and the kind of life they dream about.

Time is more precious than money; in fact, time is life because your time is up when your life comes to a halt. If time is life, then you can see how valuable this precious gift is. Each day you wake up, you should be grateful for another opportunity for the time you have and work to convert every minute into opportunities.

To dive deeper into this concept, consider reading my book, **"FIND YOUR WORK: Unlocking Your Path to Impact, Fulfilment, and Worthy Compensation,"** available at any of your favourite book outlets.

MAKE THE MOST OF EVERY CHANCE YOU GET

Time is a precious gift, and with every new day comes a fresh opportunity to make meaningful progress toward your goals. The minutes and hours that make up each day are fleeting; they can never be regained once they pass. That's why making the most of every chance you get is essential. You should count every day as another opportunity to do something meaningful. Some people wanted an extra day but were not privileged. It means you have more value to offer the world if you find yourself alive; therefore, don't waste the opportunity - make the most of every chance you get.

I remember that when I was much younger, we used to pray fervently with a verse from the Bible that says,

"redeeming the time, because the days are evil" (Ephesians 5:16). I can vividly recall the image of myself- a young boy praying that line with intense faith and energy. I had been taught that each day was filled with evil, and I genuinely believed that nothing good would come from the day unless I prayed fervently to extract any good from it. In my mind, the day held the potential for trouble and harm, and it was up to me to wrestle the good out of it through prayer.

Over the years, I realised that while it's important to acknowledge that challenges and difficulties exist, focusing solely on the "evil" of the day limits my perspective. Why was I so consumed by the idea of the day being filled with evil rather than seeing the potential for good that also exists in every moment? **Yes, hardships are real, but so are opportunities.** Redeeming the time is not just about praying to avoid negativity; it's about recognising that every day, despite its challenges, is filled with chances for growth, success, and fulfilment. The real question is: are we making the most of those opportunities?

As earlier said, I gained a much deeper understanding of this verse, especially when I explored it in other translations of the Bible. Imagine my surprise and how much my perspective shifted when I saw a clearer interpretation of the passage. Let me show you what I discovered by quoting the same verse from different versions. Of course, I'll begin with the version I have always known. Here is the NKJV version I grew up with: "See then that you walk circumspectly, not as fools but as wise, redeeming the time, because the days are evil. Therefore do not be unwise, but understand what the will of the Lord is."Ephesians 5:15-17

Now, let's look at two other translations that opened up new insights for me. First, here is the New Living Translation version: *"So be careful how you live. Don't live like fools, but like those who are wise.* **Make the most of every opportunity in these evil days.** *Don't act* *thoughtlessly, but understand what the Lord wants you to do."* Ephesians 5:15-17 (NLT)

And here is how it's written in The Message: *"So watch your step. Use your head.* ***Make the most of every chance you get.*** *These are desperate times! Don't live carelessly, unthinkingly. Make sure you understand what the Master wants."* Ephesians 5:15-17 (The Message)

Can you see now that redeeming the time because the days are evil means making the most of every opportunity in these evil days? Or, to put it another way—make the most of every chance you get, because these are desperate times. It's a privilege to be alive, and you should treat each day as such. The question is: will you make the most of this opportunity or waste it? **Each day should be seen as full of treasures waiting to be uncovered, much like a game with hidden rewards. If you do not**

> **Each day should be seen as full of treasures waiting to be uncovered, much like a game with hidden rewards. If you do not seek them, you will not find them.**

seek them, you will not find them. Opportunities are all around you, but you must open your eyes and mind to see and take advantage of them. **Often, the privilege or success we're looking for in distant places is right here with us—within reach. We don't always need to search elsewhere; instead, we should look inward and around us.**

Think about it: **have you ever noticed that what you focus on is what you tend to see the most? If you're always complaining or thinking about how things aren't working, that's all you'll notice.** You will see people in similar negative situations around you, which will only dampen your spirit further. It becomes a cycle of negativity, and you might miss the opportunities standing right before you. On the other hand, if you maintain a positive

> Often, the privilege or success we're looking for in distant places is right here with us—within reach. We don't always need to search elsewhere; instead, we should look inward and around us.

mindset and believe in the possibilities around you, you'll find that you start to notice those opportunities more often. **You attract what you focus on.**

Let me give you a simple example to illustrate this point. Have you ever noticed that when you start thinking about buying a particular type of phone or car, you suddenly begin to see that exact model all around you? It shows that the product has always been there, but you have never noticed it. You might now realise that your friend or neighbour already has that phone or car, and it begins to pop up everywhere you go. What's happening is that as soon as you start thinking about the product, a part of your brain, called the Reticular Activating System (RAS), begins to tune in and search for it. The more you focus on something, the more visible it becomes in your surroundings.

> **Have you ever noticed that what you focus on is what you tend to see the most? If you're always complaining or thinking about how things aren't working, that's all you'll notice.**

This concept works in the same way for your thoughts and mindset. If you choose to think positively, you'll start noticing and attracting positive things. You'll see opportunities, solutions, and reasons to be hopeful. On the other hand, if you focus on negativity, that's what you'll continue to see — problems, setbacks, and obstacles. So, the question becomes: which mindset would you instead cultivate? Would you prefer to attract opportunities and progress or be weighed down by negativity? The choice is entirely yours, but I encourage you to be positive and make the most of the opportunities around you.

> **You attract what you focus on.**

I love the statement that precedes the call to make the most of every opportunity in these evil days: **"So be careful how you live. Don't live like fools, but like those who are wise."** This is a crucial reminder that you must be intentional about how you live your life. You don't want to drift through life without direction or purpose, living without boundaries or goals.

Instead, you must live with intention, knowing exactly where you're heading. Being careful about how you live speaks of the importance of living purposefully, with a clear sense of direction. In these desperate times, many waste away because they don't value their time or convert it into something meaningful and productive. To avoid this pitfall, you have to deliberately choose not to join that crowd. To be successful and stand out, you must "be careful how you live."

Furthermore, the verse urges you not to live like fools but to live wisely. When you pay attention to how you spend your time, carefully accounting for each minute and ensuring it aligns with your goals, you choose the path of wisdom. Wise individuals don't allow their days to slip away aimlessly; they plan each day and stay focused on their goals. They break their long-term goals into smaller, achievable tasks they can act on daily. By doing this, they gradually see their efforts accumulate into significant results. **Success, after all, is a sum of daily efforts,** and the wise make every moment count, knowing that each step they take brings them closer to their goals.

A fool can be likened to someone who either lacks knowledge or, worse, has the knowledge but chooses not to act on it. For instance, you made the right decision to read this book, arming yourself with valuable insights about time and how to manage it effectively. The wise understand that time is a precious resource that should be invested wisely to yield meaningful dividends. They don't just acquire knowledge; they act on it, seizing the opportunities that each day presents.

> **Success, after all, is a sum of daily efforts.**

The Bible speaks of the wisdom of the children of Issachar, saying, "From the tribe of Issachar, there were 200 leaders of the tribe with their relatives. All these men understood the signs of the times and knew the best course for Israel to take" 1 Chronicles 12:32 NLT. They were considered wise because they knew and understood the seasons and took appropriate action. They had foresight and insight, which helped them give informed counsel on the course Israel should take.

Imagine living in a town with no water supply, and you've already used up the little water you had. You're not the only one—your entire neighbourhood is in the same situation. Then, you receive privileged information that a company will supply water the following week, which will be abundant. You're told you can collect as much water as you can during the supply period, but after that, there won't be any more water for the next month. Now, let's assume everyone in the town receives this information. The question is: what will you do with the information? How will you prepare for the water supply? Will you bring a single bucket, several buckets, a drum, or even go as far as

> **Response to opportunities differentiates the wise from the fool.**

creating a reservoir or dam? **Response to opportunities differentiates the wise from the fool.**

This scenario perfectly illustrates the verse: *"Don't live like fools, but like those who are wise."* A wise person sees the water supply as a limited resource, just as they view time. They understand that each day brings opportunities that won't always be there tomorrow. On the other hand, a fool may either ignore the information or bring just a small container, not realising the full potential of the situation. A wise person treats each day like a fresh water supply, engaging fully and taking advantage of every moment, while a fool allows precious opportunities to slip through their fingers without making the most of them.

Ultimately, how you approach each day defines your level of wisdom. Just as someone would prepare to store as much water as possible during a limited supply, you must treat time the same way. Each day offers a chance to invest your efforts, grow, and move closer to your goals. The wise recognise this and make every effort to maximise the value of their time. On the other hand, fools let time pass by without purpose, missing out on the opportunities that could lead to success.

Another powerful illustration of this lesson can be drawn from the story of Joseph in Egypt. Pharaoh had a troubling dream about seven fat and lean cows; none of his magicians or wise men could interpret the dream. When Joseph was summoned to interpret the dream, he explained that it was a warning from God about the future. Egypt would experience seven years of abundance, followed by seven years of severe famine. Armed with this knowledge, Joseph came up with a plan to store a portion of the surplus during the years of plenty to prepare for the coming famine.

This story illustrates the difference between living wisely and living foolishly. Joseph had foresight. He didn't just let the seven years of abundance pass by without preparation. Instead, he took action, storing grain to sustain the country through the years of famine. If Joseph and Pharaoh had ignored the dream, Egypt would have faced devastation during the famine. But because they acted on the knowledge of what was coming, Egypt survived and supplied other neighbouring nations.

Joseph's story reflects the lesson, *"Don't live like fools, but like those who are wise."* Joseph's wisdom and foresight in preparing for the future allowed him to turn a potential disaster into an opportunity for growth and leadership. Just like Joseph, you must be able to recognise opportunities when they arise and take action to prepare for the future. The wise see beyond the present moment and work diligently, knowing that preparation leads to success even in times of need. This story clearly reminds us that wisdom involves

> **Our actions should not be random or impulsive but deliberate and guided by a clear sense of purpose.**

foresight and planning, ensuring you are ready for change, crises, and the accompanying opportunities.

Here's how The Message version puts the verse we are considering, *"So be careful how you live. Don't live like fools, but like those who are wise: So watch your step. Use your head."* Is that not interesting?

The next verse, *"Don't act thoughtlessly, but understand what the Lord wants you to do,"* carries a profound message about *intentional living.* It reminds us that **our actions should not be random or impulsive but deliberate and guided by a clear sense of purpose.** Acting thoughtlessly means drifting through life without direction, making decisions without considering their long-term impact, and ultimately wasting valuable time and opportunities. This is a caution to avoid living in a reactionary manner, where you simply respond to whatever comes your way without careful consideration.

Instead, the verse urges you to *"understand what the Lord wants you to do."* This involves seeking clarity about the Creator's purpose for you and aligning your actions with that purpose. It's about taking the time to reflect, plan, and make choices that align with God's will for your life. When you have a sense of direction and purpose, your decisions are intentional, and your efforts become focused. You are no longer just going through life without direction but actively pursuing a meaningful and productive life. This verse encourages wisdom, not just in managing time, but in every aspect of your life—understanding that when you live thoughtfully and purposefully, you make the most of the opportunities presented to you.

The Message translation expresses this verse this way: *"Don't live carelessly, unthinkingly. Make sure you understand what the Master wants."* This version drives home the importance of living with purpose and intention. To live carelessly and unthinkingly is to move through life without a plan, allowing circumstances and distractions to dictate your actions. It warns against thoughtless living, where your decisions lack direction and your time is wasted on things that don't contribute to your growth or purpose.

Instead, the verse says, *"Make sure you understand what the Master wants."* This is about seeking God's guidance and aligning your choices with a higher purpose. **It's not just about being busy but about being purposeful in the things you do.** Understanding what the Master wants means living a life that is thoughtful, deliberate, and driven by a clear vision of what you're meant to accomplish. When you take the time to reflect on your purpose and commit to living it out, you stop drifting through life and start making decisions that lead to lasting success and fulfilment.

By living with intention and understanding, you avoid the pitfalls of careless living. You start to make the most of every opportunity and use your time wisely, knowing that every action counts. This approach ensures success and aligns your life with a greater purpose, giving your efforts deeper meaning and impact.

As we conclude this chapter, it becomes clear that time is one of our most precious resources. Each moment is an opportunity—an invitation to create, grow, and move closer to your goals. Whether it's making the most of each day, avoiding distractions, or living with purpose, how you spend your time will determine the course of your life and success.

Reflect, Adjust, and Take Action

As we conclude this chapter, it's time to translate these insights into action. Take a moment for a practical self-assessment:

1. Review how you have spent your time over the last seven days. List your most significant activities and habits.

2. Evaluate whether the above activities align with the excellence and success you envision. If you continue on this path, will you achieve your goals?
3. Identify the adjustments you need to make. Perhaps it's dedicating more time to learning, eliminating distractions, or being more deliberate about structuring your day.

Time is a precious gift that cannot be reclaimed. Whatever adjustments you identify, commit to taking immediate action. **Start small if necessary, but start now.** Your future self will thank you for making the most of the gift of time today.

> **Start small if necessary, but start now.**

As vital as time is, there is something just as essential: your thoughts. Time alone, without the fuel of thinking, will not yield results. In the next chapter, "The Power of Thoughts: Nothing Meaningful Happens Without It," we will explore the power of the mind—how your thoughts, ideas, and mental focus are the starting point for all success. Just as time must be invested wisely, so must your thoughts. Get ready to unlock the next step in your journey because, without positive thought, nothing meaningful happens.

CHAPTER THREE

The Power of Thoughts: Nothing Meaningful Happens Without It

"By faith we understand that the entire universe was formed at God's command, that what we now see did not come from anything that can be seen." Heb 11:3

Every outstanding achievement, invention, or discovery begins with a single thought. All the wonders we see around us stem from the unseen realm of ideas, and it is often said that what we see originates from what we do not see. The unseen world—the world of thoughts and creativity—holds untold riches and potential. Imagine how meaningful and impactful your life could be if you could mine this unseen world to its fullest. **Thoughts are the seeds of greatness; they shape your attitude, influence your behaviour, and drive your actions.** Your thoughts hold the power to determine the trajectory of your life. Without them, progress or creation is impossible. As Napoleon Hill aptly stated, *"Whatever the mind can conceive and believe, it can achieve."* This truth highlights the immense power within your capacity to think. Engaging in mental or brain work is arguably the most meaningful effort you can undertake, as it sets the foundation for your horizons and possibilities.

> Every outstanding achievement, invention, or discovery begins with a single thought.

In this chapter, we will explore the critical role that thought plays in shaping our lives. Just as the gift of time requires intentionality

> Thoughts are the seeds of greatness; they shape your attitude, influence your behaviour, and drive your actions.

to transform it into success, so does the power of thought demand your attention and mastery. Together, we'll uncover how harnessing this incredible resource can unlock success in the various aspects of your life—whether it be in your finances, relationships, career, or personal growth. Let us get started.

IS IT A CRIME TO THINK?

As a medical doctor, I often hear patients attribute their high blood pressure to thinking. They say, *"I have high blood pressure because I think too much."* This always leaves me wondering how the act of thinking—a fundamental human function—could be blamed for causing hypertension. Could it be that they are confusing thinking with worrying or anxiety? Positive thinking, after all, has been shown to promote physical health. Yet, many people reduce this powerful, life-transforming ability to a cause of illness, misunderstanding its true potential. They view what could elevate and empower them as a source of harm, failing to distinguish between productive thinking and the burdens of anxiety.

The truth is, as long as you are alive and your brain is functioning, you will think. The question is not whether you think but what kind of thoughts dominate your mind. Are they constructive or destructive? Are they nurturing or draining? Positive thinking can be an incredible tool for creativity, problem-solving, and growth, while negative thoughts can lead to stagnation and despair. To attribute high blood pressure to thinking itself is ironic because such an attribution is, in fact, a thought. We should instead master our thoughts and harness its transformative power. After all, **the power to shape your life lies not in the absence of thought but in the quality of your thought.** So, is it really a crime to think—or is it an

> **The power to shape your life lies not in the absence of thought but in the quality of your thought.**

avenue to harness the transformative power of your mind?

Being anxious is often the result of dwelling on negative or worrisome thoughts. When such thoughts dominate your mind for extended periods, they can manifest in your physical body, affecting your health. This is why the counsel to *"be anxious for nothing, but in everything by prayer and supplication, with thanksgiving, let your requests be made known to God"* is so powerful. Prayer and supplication are not just acts of faith but also a way of redirecting your thoughts toward hope, gratitude, and solutions. **Prayer and supplication are, in themselves, forms of thoughts - engaging them creates space for clarity, solution, peace, and motivation.** Rather than allowing anxiety to control your thoughts, prayer and supplication transform them into avenues of reflection and problem-solving, revealing opportunities hidden within the challenges. **Challenges do not walk alone; they go alongside opportunities.** What would you like to focus on - the challenges or the opportunities?

The key to overcoming anxiety lies in how you think. Solutions to life's challenges are often found within the seed of your thoughts. Positive, intentional thinking can uncover possibilities and bring about the change you desire. When your thoughts are constructive, they guide your actions toward a solution, and when combined with prayer, they instil a sense of peace and purpose. **Thinking is not a crime — it is a gift.** By mastering the art of positive thought, you can transform your challenges into stepping stones for growth and success.

> Challenges do not walk alone; they go alongside opportunities.

Prayer need not be a display of emotion, ritual, or religion. It is not about shouting, screaming, banging your head, crying, or adopting a seemingly holy or religious posture; instead, it is as simple as having a conversation—a conversation with your Creator.

Do you shout or scream at someone when you want to converse with them? Or do you bang your head against a wall to get their attention? Or do you assume an awkward posture just to chat with a friend? Of course not. Yet, this is exactly what many people do when they attempt to communicate with their Creator—they shout, scream, and take on dramatic religious postures at the slightest opportunity. Communicating with your Creator should be as natural and straightforward as speaking to a close friend or a loving father who is always eager to listen and respond. After all, true communication is a two-way process: it involves both speaking and listening. Don't speak alone, listen too!

When faced with challenges, prayer allows you to focus on seeking solutions rather than grumbling or venting frustrations. Many people mistake complaining for praying—they list grievances and recount every misfortune but never open their minds to receive insights or guidance. They desire an immediate end to their struggles but are unwilling to embrace the lessons or opportunities those struggles might present. True prayer invites a shift in perspective, helping you see the possibilities hidden within the adversity.

Complaints such as "If only I were born into a better family," "Why am I not as fortunate as others?" or "Why is this happening to me?" are rooted in self-pity and despair. These thoughts offer no solution and often deepen feelings of helplessness. Instead, consider praying with a mindset of hope and discovery: "Lord, I acknowledge that I am in a difficult situation, but I trust that every challenge carries an opportunity for growth and impact. Please help me see the hidden opportunities in this challenge. Grant me the wisdom to recognise the resources and help I need, and guide me to take the right actions to emerge stronger, wiser, and more successful." This shift from complaint to constructive meditation empowers your thoughts to work for you rather than against you.

Jesus knew the suffering He would face on the cross while He was on earth. It's natural for anyone, even the Son of God, to wish to avoid pain. Jesus saw the agony of the crucifixion and prayed fervently, desiring that it might pass from Him. Yet, He surrendered, saying, "Let Thy will be done," because He understood the bigger picture: without the cross and its pain, humanity would not be saved. Jesus embraced the big picture, the eternal significance of His suffering. Similarly, we often fail to see beyond our immediate challenges, focusing only on what our physical eyes can perceive.

Prayer and supplication provide a lens through which we can view our circumstances from a higher perspective. They shift our focus from the immediate pain or difficulty to the opportunities and growth embedded within our trials. Through prayer, we align our thoughts with divine purpose, gaining insight and strength to navigate life's challenges. Instead of seeing obstacles as setbacks, we begin to recognise them as stepping stones to greater possibilities, enabling us to persevere with faith and hope.

There was once a young boy, the youngest of his father's sons, who spent most of his days tending sheep far from home. His isolation could easily have bred resentment; he might have wallowed in self-pity or anger toward his father and brothers for leaving him out of the family fold. But instead of allowing himself to be consumed by bitterness, he saw his solitude as an opportunity. He sharpened his skills in protecting the sheep from predators like lions and bears, honed his ability with musical instruments, and developed his gift for songwriting. The field became his training ground. Unknowing to him, these were preparing him for greatness and the future.

In time, the fruits of his diligence and mastery became evident. His exceptional skill with music led him to the royal palace to play for the king, earning him favour and recognition. But his story didn't end there. When a national crisis arose—a giant who taunted the entire nation of Israel—this boy stepped forward to solve the problem. Before doing so, he presented his "curriculum vitae," recounting how he killed the lion and the bear while he was in the field to protect his flock, demonstrating that his time spent in obscurity was not wasted but was instead a period of preparation.

This young shepherd was none other than David, who later became one of the greatest kings in Israel. His journey teaches us the power of viewing challenges as opportunities for growth. Rather than dwelling on his difficult circumstances, David used them as stepping stones to build the character, skills, and courage he needed for his future. His story

> **Even in the most unlikely situations, there is a divine purpose at work.**

reminds us that **even in the most unlikely situations, there is a divine purpose at work.**

EMBRACE YOUR DIVINE NATURE.

As we have seen previously, thinking is not a crime but a divine gift. Besides, nothing meaningful happens without thinking. It is the starting point for creativity, innovation, and problem-solving. **Mastering your thoughts for creation and innovation makes you embrace your nature, which is nothing short of divine, and that is why your potential is unlimited.**

Deepak Chopra wrote about *"The Law of Pure Potentiality"* in his book, The Seven Spiritual Laws of Success, emphasising the boundless possibilities inherent within every individual. According to this principle, at the core of our being lies pure consciousness, a field of infinite potential. This law illustrates that every person has access to an unbounded source of creativity, abundance, and fulfilment. By tapping into this state of pure awareness—free from fear, judgement, and external limitations—we can harness the infinite potential to shape our realities and achieve outstanding success.

To harness the Law of Pure Potentiality, one must master meditation and self-awareness, which quieten the outside world's noise and open up a space for creativity. This law demonstrates the power of your thoughts. Additionally, practising non-judgment helps maintain a sense of openness to possibilities. Do you know why many achieve below their capacity? One of the reasons is that they judge their ability - they see themselves as unworthy and incapable. Therefore, practising non-judgement to our ability opens us up to possibilities we will naturally not embrace. Do you remember the story of Gideon, who was called a mighty man of valour by the angel, but he did not identify himself as such?

> **When we align ourselves with the law of pure potentiality, we unlock a life of limitless opportunities.**

When we align ourselves with the law of pure potentiality, we unlock a life of limitless opportunities.

I was teaching a group of students and asked if they could memorise a portion of what I was teaching. Almost everyone said no, and I could see on their faces that they felt the passage was too long to memorise. Then, I offered a monetary gift to anyone who could learn it within a few minutes. Their faces lit up almost instantly, and they embraced the challenge of learning it.

What do you think happened here? They have the capacity to learn the passage, as we know that the human brain is incredibly powerful, but they initially refuse to embrace their ability. Why? Because they judged their potential and shut themselves down. Don't shut yourself down!

Imagine what you would attain and achieve if you could stop being judgmental about who you are and what you can imagine, think, or achieve—you'll unlock a vast world of possibilities for yourself.

When you master your thoughts for creation, innovation, and problem-solving, you take after the Creator Himself, who demonstrated the power of thoughts in the creation story. *"In the beginning, God created the heavens and the earth. The earth was without form and void, and darkness was over the face of the deep."*[9] This description vividly depicts a chaotic, disorganised and messy world—a problem waiting for a solution. The way the Message Version puts it is interesting. Here is it: *" First this: God created the Heavens and Earth — all you see, all you don't see. Earth was a soup of nothingness, a bottomless emptiness, an inky blackness. God's Spirit brooded like a bird above the watery abyss."*

But instead of abandoning the earth to its state or blaming anyone for the mess, it was said that the Spirit of God hovers over the face of the waters. The Hebrew word, *rachaph*, translated *to hover*, also means *"brood"*, which describes what the Spirit of God was doing - the

Spirit of God was brooding much like a bird sitting on its eggs, nurturing them to life. This act of brooding is a powerful metaphor for meditation. It involves careful, focused thought—a deep engagement of the mind to birth solutions and new realities. Just as a bird's patient brooding eventually produces visible chicks, your mastery of thoughts will lead to tangible results. There is no way you will master your thoughts that there would not be a result.

This practice of brooding is not passive but active, intentional, and purposeful. It requires time, focus, and persistence. Just as God brought order and beauty out of chaos, you can use the power of your thoughts to bring clarity, direction, and success into your life. By mastering your thoughts, you can turn ideas into impactful realities that are not only visible to you but beneficial to the world around you.

> **God thinks; if He does, we should.**

As likened to meditation, the Spirit of God hovering over the face of the waters shows us the profound importance of thoughts. It also shows **that God thinks; if He does, we should.** God is a thinker, as reinforced by Jeremiah when he reported that God thinks about you. He thinks about how to set you up for great, undeniable success. *"'For I know the thoughts that I think toward you,' says the LORD, 'thoughts of peace and not of evil, to give you a future and a hope.'"*[22]

This further emphasises that God is a thinker and it is never a crime to think: *"'For My thoughts are not your thoughts, Nor are your ways My ways,' says the LORD. 'For as the heavens are higher than the earth, So are My ways higher than your ways, And My thoughts than your thoughts.'"*[23]

If God Himself begins the act of creation with deep thoughts, how much more should we, as His creations, embrace the power of thoughts? Without this meditative process, the order and beauty that followed would not have come into existence. This reinforces a timeless truth: nothing meaningful happens without first harnessing the power of your thoughts. If you desire to transform your situation or elevate your life, the starting point is your mind - if you want to change your life, then change your thoughts.

When God emerged from His meditation, His first words were, *"Let there be light."* This is a profound lesson in prioritisation and organisation. God did not begin with plants, animals, or any other part of creation. Light came first because it was essential for everything else to thrive.

In the same way, thinking brings clarity, order, and direction to your life. It enables you to plan, prioritise, and create a foundation upon which success can be built. Just as God's thought preceded creation, your thoughts must lead the way for meaningful changes in your journey.

It is interesting to know that the light God called into being at the start of creation wasn't the sun, moon, or stars—these came later. Instead, this light can be understood as a symbol of knowledge, clarity, and enlightenment. It was the foundation upon which everything else in creation was built. This highlights an essential principle: **before any meaningful progress can occur in life, you must first seek clarity and understanding.** Life can feel directionless and uninspiring without clarity, much like a journey without a map. Embracing knowledge and clarity helps you uncover your purpose, which becomes the guiding light that fuels your motivation and energises your efforts.

When you harness the power of thought, you create your own *'light'* — the clarity that illuminates your path in life. This light brings purpose to your personal and professional endeavours, strengthens your relationships, and empowers your financial and spiritual growth. Just as God's light ushered in the creation of all things, your clarity and understanding will pave the way for remarkable accomplishments in every area of your life.

When you begin to engage the power of your thoughts, it is essential to remember that results may not be immediately visible. This can feel discouraging, but just like the bird that patiently broods over its eggs, a process quietly unfolds beneath the surface. From the very first day of brooding, changes begin to occur within the egg—changes that are not visible to the naked eye but are essential for the eventual hatching of a live chick. Similarly, your initial efforts in harnessing the power of your thoughts set a process in motion. Though these early stages may not produce immediate tangible outcomes, they are crucial for the transformation and success that lies ahead.

> **Greatness often requires incubation—a period of unseen growth and preparation.**

Patience and consistency are key during this phase. Trust the process and continue to nurture your thoughts with positivity. **Greatness often requires incubation—a period of unseen growth and preparation.** Just because you cannot yet see the results does not mean progress isn't being made. As you persevere, your consistent engagement with the power of thought will eventually yield evident and impactful outcomes, just as the chick emerges from the egg after a period of brooding.

When I was much younger, we used to rear hens, and I vividly recall a lesson learned from those experiences. Sometimes, we would take eggs from under a brooding hen,

> Just because change isn't visible on the surface doesn't mean transformation isn't taking place.

thinking they were still regular eggs. We would boil and crack them open, only to discover that parts of a chick had already started forming inside the shell. To us, the eggs seemed unchanged from the outside, but in reality, the process of development had begun the very moment the hen started brooding. This revealed a profound truth: **just because change isn't visible on the surface doesn't mean transformation isn't taking place.**

This is an illustration of the process of engaging your thoughts. At first, it may feel like nothing is happening—as if the effort you're investing in creative thinking, problem-solving, or planning is yielding no visible results. But just as the hen's persistent brooding sparks unseen development within the egg, your consistent and focused thoughts initiate an internal transformation. Trust that progress is happening even when it isn't immediately apparent because growth and change often begin in places hidden from view.

Building on our earlier discussion on prayers and supplication, it's important to recognise that the answers to prayers often come in the form of ideas—what I like to call strategies. These ideas might not seem grand or miraculous at first glance, but they carry the seeds of the solutions you seek. The true mark of wisdom lies in recognising these ideas for what they are and acting upon them. Just as faith without works is dead, prayers without action remain unfruitful. Acting on these divinely inspired strategies is a demonstration of faith and trust.

I elaborated further on this subject in one of my books, **"From Debt to Wealth: 12 Keys to Earning Money with What You Have."** Here are the links to get the book: https://link.pnuxelconsulting.com/fdtwa or https://pnuxelconsulting.com/fdtwe

WOULD YOU LIKE TO EARN MORE?

The evolution of work tells a fascinating story. The Agricultural Age, which lasted for centuries, involved human labour centred around agriculture, where survival was tied to muscle power and the ability to cultivate the land. By the early 19th century, officially 1815, the Industrial Age emerged, bringing machinery and mass production into the picture. This era, defined by manufacturing and factory work, lasted about 150 years before the Service Age took over. By 1960, delivering services became the dominant form of work, marking a significant shift in how people earned their livelihoods. Yet, this phase was remarkably brief; by the 1980s, the world had transitioned into the Information Age, and before long, we entered the Age of Communication, where we now reside. **Each shift has happened more rapidly than the last, underlining the speed at which the world of work continues to evolve.**

In today's Communication Age, the value of labour lies not in physical strength or repetitive tasks but in ideas, knowledge, and the ability to share them effectively. **We have moved from the use of brute power to brainpower, from moving things to moving ideas.** The emphasis is now on creativity, communication, and the ability to connect with others meaningfully, which could be described as the **"triple C"**. Your success—financially, professionally, and personally—is now directly tied to your ability to generate and communicate valuable ideas.

This shift carries a powerful lesson: **to earn more, you must think differently and adapt to the demands of the age you live in.** Gone are the days when long hours of physical labour guaranteed success. **Today, what sets people apart is their ability to harness their intellect, leverage technology, and deliver unique solutions to modern problems.** This is why some earn exponentially more than others—they understand the importance of positioning themselves in the flow of new opportunities created by the Communication Age.

> To earn more, you must think differently and adapt to the demands of the age you live in.

> Today, what sets people apart is their ability to harness their intellect, leverage technology, and deliver unique solutions to modern problems.

If you've ever wondered how to raise your earning potential, it begins with embracing this reality. **Your ability to generate, process, share, and implement valuable ideas has become the currency of the modern economy.**

In this age, where ideas and innovation reign, thinkers are the true game-changers. They are paid more because the real wealth is created in the mind before it is ever seen in the physical world.

> Today's most valuable companies don't rely on massive factories or expansive lands; instead, they thrive on the intellectual capital of individuals—ideas born in the minds of creative, forward-thinking people.

Today's most valuable companies don't rely on massive factories or expansive lands; instead, they thrive on the intellectual capital of individuals—ideas born in the minds of creative,

forward-thinking people. A billion-dollar company can now exist as a concept within the mind of someone walking down the street whose outward appearance might not even hint at the treasure they carry. This underscores the immense potential locked within your thoughts and imagination.

If you want to earn more, the key lies in paying attention to your mind and harnessing its power. Increase what you know, and more importantly, learn how to apply that knowledge to solve real-world problems. The more value you can create through your ideas and solutions, the higher your earning capacity. In this era, those who master their minds—who think deeply, innovate, and act decisively—are the ones who consistently rise above the rest. You position yourself not just to survive but to

The Power of Thoughts: Nothing Meaningful Happens Without It

thrive in a world driven by the currency of ideas by intentionally nurturing your mental capacities.

Knowledge, understanding, and wisdom are crucial, but it is wisdom—the practical application of knowledge and understanding—that truly creates value. **Simply accumulating knowledge in your field isn't enough to increase your income or improve your financial standing. The key lies in applying what you know to solve real, pressing problems in ways that make a tangible difference.** This is the principle that separates those who merely possess information from those who thrive financially and professionally. Without actively using your knowledge to address challenges, your earning

> If you want to earn more, the key lies in paying attention to your mind and harnessing its power. Increase what you know, and more importantly, learn how to apply that knowledge to solve real-world problems.

potential will remain stagnant or even diminish over time.

Alarming, many people fail even to embrace knowledge, let alone apply it. They remain stuck, not because they lack potential but because they refuse to expand their knowledge and take meaningful action. If you want to increase your earning power, you must not only pursue learning but also look for ways to translate that learning into practical solutions. Those who combine knowledge, understanding, and the boldness to apply what they have learnt are the ones who consistently rise to new heights of success.

> **Simply accumulating knowledge in your field isn't enough to increase your income or improve your financial standing. The key lies in applying what you know to solve real, pressing problems in ways that make a tangible difference.**

It is often said that knowledge is power - it is a misconception that simply acquiring knowledge guarantees power or success. **The truth is that only**

applied knowledge—knowledge used to solve problems and deliver value—carries transformative power, so applied knowledge is power. In today's economy, knowledge that translates into tangible results for others holds real value. Information that cannot be harnessed to provide a service or solve a need is often worth little, regardless of how interesting or factual it might be. This is a critical distinction that many fail to grasp, leading to frustration when their education or expertise doesn't immediately translate into financial or professional growth.

Consider this: the value of any piece of knowledge is directly tied to its usefulness in achieving results for others. Knowledge that solves problems, saves time, or enhances productivity is highly priced, as people are

> **The truth is that only applied knowledge—knowledge used to solve problems and deliver value—carries transformative power, so applied knowledge is power.**

willing to pay for the benefits they can see and experience from it.

While intellectually stimulating and true, much of what is taught in academic institutions often lacks practical application in today's fast-paced world. Many graduates are disappointed upon entering the workforce because of this gap between academic knowledge and practical utility. They quickly realise that their degrees in some fields, though impressive, are rarely sought after by employers today. **The stark reality is that 80 per cent of graduates find themselves working outside their chosen fields within two years of completing their education. The market demands problem-solvers, not merely degree-holders.** As a result, many pivots to roles where they can develop skills that are immediately valuable to others.

After graduating from medical school, I quickly realised that having a degree—even one as esteemed as medicine—was not enough for financial success. I was partially shielded from this reality during my one-year compulsory internship because the institutions were obligated to take in medical interns and provide us with a stipend. However, once that year ended and I started looking for a job to support myself and my new family, the truth hit me hard - securing the job wasn't about my degree but about the problems I could solve.

> **The stark reality is that 80 per cent of graduates find themselves working outside their chosen fields within two years of completing their education. The market demands problem-solvers, not merely degree-holders.**

From one interview to the other, it was clear that emphasis was not placed on my qualifications but on what I could do. After all, everyone who was present at the interview had the certificate. Are you proficient with such and such procedures? How many times have you performed the procedure? These were a few of the common questions at the interviews. It dawned on me that employers were looking for people who could help keep their establishments running *efficiently and profitably*—not just someone with a fancy degree. This rude awakening forced me to adjust my mindset quickly. I had to accept that **life operates on the principle of value exchange: you cannot expect something for nothing.** Looking back, I can see that many graduates face the same challenge. If they had known earlier, perhaps they would have approached their studies differently—choosing fields with practical applications, seeking the application of what they

> **Life operates on the principle of value exchange: you cannot expect something for nothing.**

learned in school or acquiring additional skills along the way.

During my university years at the Obafemi Awolowo University, Ile-Ife, I remember there was an event titled **Beyond Ife,** if my memory served me right. The theme intrigued me, as it aimed to prepare students for the realities awaiting them after graduation. But, like many others, I was too engrossed in my medical books and other things of personal interest. It wasn't until after school that I understood the message they were trying to convey: life after university is much more than the certificate you earn—it's about the value you bring to the table. Looking back, I wish I had attended that event. Perhaps it would have spared me some of the hard lessons I later had to learn about life outside the protective walls of academia. I think right from the first year in college; students should be educated about the reality of the world after school so that they can adequately prepare.

Interestingly, while my medical education laid a foundation, my journey after university has been enriched by other skills I picked up along the way. Beyond medicine, I discovered a love for writing and publishing—a skill that has not only increased my earning potential but also enabled me to bring value to others. This book you're reading is one such example. Writing wasn't something I initially planned to build a business or service around, but as I honed my craft, I realised it was a tool to meet the needs of others. Over time, I began teaching people how to write and publish books, assisting people with publishing and even ventured into ghostwriting. Alongside writing, I ventured into learning web design and other digital skills, all while improving my medical expertise.

Today, as a dermatology resident on the path to becoming a specialist, I can confidently say that honing these skills has been very useful and a great decision I made. Whether related to medicine or not, each skill has added layers of value to my personal and professional journey. It's a lesson I hope will inspire others to explore their interests, embrace lifelong learning, and consider the value they can offer the world.

Focusing on acquiring and applying knowledge that addresses real needs is essential to thrive in this competitive world. It's not just about learning—it's about learning with purpose. By continuously seeking to understand what others need and finding ways to meet those needs with your knowledge, you position yourself to earn more, grow more, and make a meaningful impact. Remember, in this age of communication, the ability to apply what you know to create solutions is the currency.

THINKERS AND STRATEGISTS ARE PAID MORE.

As a high school student, I often observed an intriguing contrast during my walks home each afternoon. I would pass by men, some muscular and others not necessarily so, working tirelessly under the scorching sun. These men dug tunnels, carried heavy loads, and laboured on construction sites or in the bustling markets, offloading cement or transporting goods from one place to another. Their hard work was evident, yet they were not wealthy - it is obvious that they were not. It puzzled me—why were these men, who worked so hard, often paid so little compared to others in cool, air-conditioned offices or luxurious cars?

Over time, I came to understand the root of this paradox. The world of work is divided into two broad categories: physical labour and mental work. Most of the men I saw were engaged in physically demanding tasks, often executing the plans and ideas conceived by others who used their mental capacity. Mental work, though less visibly tasking, requires a different kind of energy—foresight, creativity, strategic thinking, and the courage to carry out the ideas. I hope you know that it takes courage to embark on an idea, especially one you have never implemented before - you are not perfectly sure if it will work. This invisible labour, mental work, is what shapes industries, drives innovation, and ultimately commands higher rewards.

Mental work is not without its challenges. It involves taking risks, planning meticulously, and often failing multiple times before succeeding. In fact, most ideas fail before one breakthrough idea emerges. But when that breakthrough comes, the rewards are substantial, often compensating for the many failed attempts. This underscores why thinkers and strategists are valued so highly. They possess the ability to foresee possibilities, craft strategies, and turn ideas into reality—a process that requires a remarkable blend of resilience, courage, intellect, and vision.

> **If you aspire to earn more, elevate your mental game. Develop your capacity to think strategically, innovate boldly, and execute effectively and fearlessly.**

The premium placed on mental work has never been higher in our current age. We are in a time where ideas are the currency of success, and their implementation is what sets people apart. Thinkers and strategists envision possibilities and create value that others are willing to pay for. The lesson here is clear: **if you aspire to earn more, elevate your mental game. Develop your capacity to think strategically, innovate boldly, and execute effectively and fearlessly.** This is how you position yourself for greater compensation and lasting impact.

Another crucial factor to consider is the immense amount of training and commitment required to become a skilled thinker or strategist. **Expertise in any field doesn't happen overnight.** Take, for instance, the difference between a butcher and a surgeon. While it may take only weeks or months to learn the skills necessary to become a butcher, it takes many years of rigorous education, training, and practice to become a surgeon. This disparity in time investment and the complexity of the work directly influences their compensation. A surgeon's work involves much more mental work, precision, and responsibility, justifying the significantly higher pay.

Even among surgeons, the time and effort required can vary significantly based on their speciality. For example, a general surgeon and a spine surgeon follow vastly different paths, with the latter requiring additional years of training and specialisation. The same principle applies across professions and industries. Those who dedicate themselves to acquiring knowledge and refining their expertise often command higher compensation. Their ability to navigate complex challenges and offer unique solutions makes their contributions invaluable in today's economy. This reinforces why thinkers and strategists invest heavily in their mental development and are compensated more generously.

A typical example of the power of mental work can be seen in Joseph's life in Egypt. Joseph's ability to interpret Pharaoh's dreams and devise a strategy to save Egypt from impending famine was a mental feat of extraordinary value. His solution addressed a national crisis, and he was compensated accordingly, rising to the position of second-in-command in Egypt. In contrast, the labourers who gathered and stored the grain worked physically hard, often in challenging conditions. Yet, despite their essential contribution, their compensation could never rival Joseph's because his mental work—his insight and strategy—made the entire operation possible.

This principle underscores the enduring truth that mental work holds greater value because it drives progress, solves problems, and creates opportunities. Even today, your thoughts and ideas have the potential to transform your life. Your mind is your richest resource, capable of producing incredible results when tapped into and cultivated. If you seek to change any aspect of your life—whether it's your finances, relationships, or career—you must begin with your mindset. Change your thoughts, align them with your goals, and commit to the necessary work. If you can believe it and are ready to put in the work required, you will be surprised by how much you can achieve. Do not forget that nothing meaningful happens if you do not think.

THE PHYSICAL WORLD IS AN EXPRESSION OF THE INVISIBLE WORLD

Which of these worlds is the real world: the visible or the invisible? While it may seem obvious to assume that the tangible, physical world is more "real," the truth is far more profound. There is far more happening in the unseen realm than in the seen. Take a moment to consider your current surroundings. What can you see? Now, think about what exists around you that you cannot see. Countless living organisms—microorganisms—are moving and functioning without your physical eyes detecting them. The air you breathe, the signals

> **Your physical world is an expression of your invisible world**

transmitting information to your devices, and even the gravitational force keeping you seated are all invisible yet undeniably real. The invisible world is as much a part of your reality as the visible one.

From the very beginning, creation itself has pointed to this profound truth. In the account of Genesis, we read, *"In the beginning, God created the heavens and the earth."* Notice the distinction: 'heavens' is plural, indicating multiple realms or dimensions of existence, while 'earth' is singular, confined to the physical realm. The physical world is but an expression or a shadow of the realities of the invisible world. Everything we see, touch, and interact with results from unseen processes, forces, and ideas that brought it into existence.

This perspective has practical implications. If the physical world is shaped by the invisible, then to bring about change in the visible world, one must first engage with the unseen realm—thoughts, beliefs, ideas, and principles. These intangible elements are the source of all creation and innovation. You activate the unseen forces that shape reality by aligning your internal world with your desired outcomes.

The invisible world could rightly be called the "real world," as nothing in the physical realm exists or happens without the invisible world. Think for a moment about something as simple but complex as raising your hand. You see the physical act of movement, but countless invisible processes are at work beneath the surface. Impulses are generated in your brain, electrical signals travel through your nervous system, and chemicals are released in your muscles, all unseen, yet essential to the visible action. The physical world is merely a manifestation of these unseen processes.

The Bible states, *"By faith we understand that the universe was formed at God's command,* **so that what is seen was not made out of what was visible"** *Hebrews 11:3, NIV.* Everything we observe in the physical world originates from the invisible. God, the ultimate Creator, used the unseen to bring the seen into existence. Similarly, humans operate under the same principle in their creative processes. In his book, The 7 Habits of Highly Effective People, Stephen Covey describes this concept as the "two creations." Every tangible creation is first imagined, planned, or designed in the mind before it takes its physical form.

Consider the buildings you walk past, the devices you use, or the music you enjoy. Each of these began as an invisible idea, a concept that someone visualised in their mind. The creation process starts in the unseen realm of thoughts, beliefs, and ideas, which are then translated into physical reality through effort and action. Recognising this principle empowers us to focus more on nurturing our invisible world—the realm of thoughts and imagination—because it is the source of everything we hope to achieve or become.

Stephen Covey introduces the idea of mental and physical creations. This principle illustrates that all things are created twice—first in the mind and then in the physical realm. Just as a building follows a blueprint, our physical manifestations are preceded by mental conceptions. Covey emphasises the importance of beginning with the end in mind, utilising the power of imagination to envision what we desire before bringing it into existence.

So, to shape your physical reality, you must first engage the power of your mind—the unseen world that serves as the blueprint for everything you see and experience. The world around you is a reflection of your thoughts, beliefs, and ideas. If you hope for a future filled with success, abundance, and impact, you must first create it in your mind. This is why faith is so powerful; it acts as the fuel that propels your thoughts into action and brings your ideas into reality. As Henry Ford aptly said, *"If you think you can do a thing or think you can't do a thing, you're right."* Your mindset sets the boundaries of what is possible in your life.

Napoleon Hill reinforced this truth, declaring, *"You can do it if you believe you can."* Every breakthrough, every invention, and every life-changing moment began as a thought. Your ability to harness and channel the power of your mind determines how far you can go. **The question is not whether you are capable but whether you are willing to engage your thoughts, nurture your belief, and take the actions needed to translate your invisible ideas into visible success.**

As we conclude this chapter, it is clear that the unseen forces of thought, belief, and imagination shape your physical world. Your ability to harness these invisible elements is the key to creating your desired life. Every innovation, achievement, and success begins in the mind, making it your most valuable resource.

> **The question is not whether you are capable but whether you are willing to engage your thoughts, nurture your belief, and take the actions needed to translate your invisible ideas into visible success.**

But how do you maximise this extraordinary gift? How can you transform the power of your thoughts into tangible outcomes and lasting success? The next chapter, How to Leverage the Richest Mine, will show you practical ways to tap into the wealth of your mind. You'll discover strategies to unlock your potential, convert your ideas into reality, and elevate your life.

The richest mine is waiting for you to explore. Let's uncover its treasures together. Turn the page and take the next step in your journey to greatness.

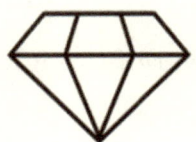

Chapter Four

How to Leverage the Richest Mine

"The best way to predict the future is to create it." — Abraham Lincoln

Congratulations on making it this far! By journeying through the pages of this book, you've demonstrated your commitment to self-discovery, growth, and the pursuit of success. We uncovered some of life's profound truths in the previous chapters. Chapter One revealed the extraordinary potential within you, introducing the concept of the richest mine and its boundless treasures. Chapter Two illuminated the gift of time, showing you how to value and transform this irreplaceable resource into success. Chapter Three built on this foundation, highlighting the power of thought and its pivotal role in shaping your lives.

Now, we are at the final chapter, where the focus shifts from understanding to action. This chapter will explore practical strategies to unearth, refine, and apply the wealth within. This chapter is your pass to converting insights into impact, transforming dreams into reality, and achieving the success you've always envisioned. Prepare to take the tools you've gathered and put them to work—because the richest mine is ready to yield its treasures to those who dare to act because nothing happens if you do not act.

AUTOMATING YOUR JOURNEY TO SUCCESS

Let me begin this section by drawing on a personal experience that amazed me of the power of the human mind. I have a routine of picking up my children from school and driving them home along a familiar route. One day, while heading to pick them up from school, I found myself lost in thought—and, without realising it, I ended up navigating the route to their school without giving it a thought. It was as if my mind had switched to autopilot.

When I realised what had happened, I was struck by the mind's incredible capacity to automate actions. Even though I was deep in thought, I didn't lose my way. This illustrates how incredibly powerful the mind is. Imagine applying this principle to your journey towards success—programming your mind so thoroughly with the habits and beliefs needed for growth that they become second nature and automatic.

Repetition is the tool that engrains these patterns into our subconscious. I could navigate the road when I was lost in thought because I had taken the route several times. By consistently practising the right habits, making deliberate choices, and focusing on success-oriented thoughts, you can automate the behaviours and attitudes that lead to outstanding results. This isn't limited to just one area of your life. Whether it's building wealth, nurturing relationships, or advancing in your career, the principle remains the same. When you teach your mind what to focus on and practice those actions often enough, they become your default mode, propelling you towards success even without conscious effort.

Abraham Lincoln famously said, *"The best way to predict your future is to create it."* When you leverage the richest mine—your mind—you stop waiting for circumstances to align, but instead, you start creating opportunities for yourself. This is the secret behind what people often call ***"luck."*** It isn't random or accidental; instead, it is a preparation meeting with opportunity. Too often, opportunities pass unnoticed or untapped because of a lack of readiness. Leveraging your mind's power ensures that when an opportunity comes, you recognise it, seize it, and make the most of it.

Now, let's consider some practical ways to use your mind's incredible capabilities to create your desired future.

A Simple Guide On How To Leverage The Richest Mine.

1. **Acknowledge the Power of Your Mind**

    The first step to leveraging the richest mine is to recognise and embrace the immense power of your mind. Throughout this book, we have explored the mind's boundless capacity for creativity, problem-solving, and transformation. Acknowledging its vast potential is the foundation for unlocking its treasures.

    Take a moment to reflect on the fact that you can achieve far more than you have so far. Your mind holds infinite possibilities; it is a wellspring of ideas, innovation, and solutions. Embrace the truth that you are created with divine attributes and limitless potential. By recognising this, you pave the way for intentionally exploring and using your mental resources to create your desired life.

> *"Whatever the mind of man can conceive and believe, it can achieve."*
> *— Napoleon Hill.*

2. Guard the Gateways to Your Mind

Your mind is shaped by what it consumes, and your sense organs are the gateways for entrance into your mental space. What you see, hear, and feel can profoundly influence your thoughts, beliefs, and actions. It is, therefore, vital to guard these gateways diligently, for they are the conduits to your richest mine.

> **Your mind is shaped by what it consumes, and your sense organs are the gateways for entrance into your mental space.**

Imagine your mind as a fertile garden. If you allow weeds to grow unchecked, they will overgrow the flowers. In the same way, exposing your mind to negativity, harmful influences, or distractions will hinder its flourishing ability. On the other hand, feeding it with positive, uplifting, and inspiring inputs will nurture a thriving and productive mental space. For instance, the books you read, the conversations you engage in, and the media you consume shape your thought process and, consequently, your reality.

> *"Guard your heart above all else, for it determines the course of your life."*
> *— Proverbs 4:23 NLT.*

3. **Cultivate Quietness and Avoid Distractions**

In a world filled with endless noise and distractions, the ability to maintain inner quietness is crucial to leveraging your mind's vast potential. Your mind thrives in stillness, and it is in this space that clarity, creativity, and breakthrough ideas emerge. When you practice maintaining quietness, you create an environment where your mind can focus, reflect, and generate solutions to your challenges.

Think about the ocean. On the surface, there may be turbulence, but deep beneath, the waters remain calm and steady. Your mind is like that ocean. Quietness allows you to tap into its deeper layers, where the richest treasures of wisdom and insight reside. Cultivating this stillness might involve meditation, journaling, or simply taking moments to unplug from technology and social media. It's about eliminating distractions and creating a mental sanctuary where you can think without interruption.

Consider a sculptor working on a masterpiece. They require focus and an undisturbed environment to shape their vision into reality. Your mind, too, needs this kind of attentive care to mould your thoughts into success.

"The quieter you become, the more you can hear." — *Ram Dass*

4. **Practice Meditation**

   Meditation is a practice that involves focusing your mind on a subject. It is a powerful tool for unlocking the potential of your mind. It helps you declutter your thoughts, gain clarity, and channel your focus toward what truly matters. By practising meditation, you train your mind to let go of distractions and noise.

   Imagine a muddy glass of water. If you keep stirring it, the water remains cloudy, but if you let it sit still, the mud settles, and the water becomes clear. Meditation is like allowing your mind to settle; it brings clarity and helps you see your life's challenges and opportunities with a fresh perspective.

   There's no one-size-fits-all method for meditation. You can learn to disengage from the hustle and bustle of each day to maintain quietness and a time to think and visualise the kind of life you want.

> *"Keep this Book of the Law always on your lips; **meditate on it day and night**, so that you may be careful to do everything written in it. **Then you will be prosperous and successful."** Joshua 1:8 NIV*

When your mind is calm and focused, you are better equipped to make decisions, solve problems, and create your desired future.

5. Learn to Document Your Thoughts, Inspirations, Ideas, Goals, and Aspirations

The act of writing down your thoughts and ideas is a powerful step in leveraging your mind's riches. Once an idea has taken shape in your mind, the next crucial step is to document it. This involves writing down every detail of the idea, no matter how insignificant it

> **The faintest ink is said to be better than the strongest memory, so documentation is crucial.**

initially seems. Documentation serves several essential purposes. It helps you organise your thoughts and see the idea more clearly, which can reveal aspects of it that you may not have initially considered. Writing down your idea also creates a record that you can refer back to, helping you track its evolution over time and your progress. **The faintest ink is said to be better than the strongest memory, so documentation is crucial.**

A well-documented idea could also be a communication tool when you need to share your idea with others, such as potential partners, investors, or team members. It can help prevent misconceptions and ensure everyone understands the concept clearly, reducing the risk of miscommunication as you turn your idea into a valuable asset.

Think of your mind as a vast, fertile land. Ideas are like seeds that need to be planted in the right place to grow. Writing them down can be likened to sowing seeds as it allows you to see what you need to nurture easily.

Keep a journal, notebook, or digital app handy to record your ideas, no matter how small they may seem.

> *"The faintest ink is more powerful than the strongest memory."* —
> *Chinese Proverb.*

By documenting your goals and aspirations, you also create a sense of accountability and a visual reminder of what you're working toward. Regularly revisit these writings to track your progress, make adjustments, and stay inspired. In doing so, you actively participate in the creation of your success, turning your thoughts into actions and your actions into achievements.

6. Clarify and Refine Your Ideas

Understand the core value of your idea. What problem does it intend to solve? Who will benefit from it? Determine who will benefit from your idea. Understand their needs, preferences, and pain points. The better you understand your target audience, the more effectively you can tailor your idea to meet their demands.

You may also examine similar products or services in the market, learning from their successes and mistakes. This will help you position your idea uniquely and avoid potential pitfalls.

Make sure you can articulate the details of your idea clearly. Refine it until it comes to taste. Do not be discouraged at the first sketch because it is not likely to be perfect at the beginning, but continue to clarify and refine until it comes to taste. Also, you do not have to wait until everything is perfect before you start working on the idea. You can always refine along the way.

> *"The best way to have a good idea is to have a lot of ideas."* — Linus Pauling.

7. Confess Your Goals with Confidence

Writing your goals is an essential step, but declaring them to yourself takes it to another level. When you consistently speak your goals in the form of positive affirmations, you reinforce them in your subconscious mind, which plays a vital role in shaping your reality. Speaking your goals transforms them from abstract ideas into tangible aspirations, setting your mental focus and energy on achieving them.

For instance, imagine a young athlete aspiring to win a championship. By repeatedly affirming, "I am a champion," they boost their confidence and train their mind to focus on the behaviours and habits required to achieve that title. This principle applies to any area of life — be it your career, finances, or relationships.

When crafting your declarations or affirmations, it is essential to phrase them in the positive form. This is because the subconscious mind does not process negative statements effectively and tends to focus on the main subject of the statement. For example, saying "I am not poor" could inadvertently reinforce the notion of poverty in your mind, as the subconscious mind picks up on the word "poor" rather than the "not."

Instead, reframe your affirmations positively by focusing on what you want to achieve. For instance, say, "I am wealthy" or "I attract abundance into my life." Such affirmations resonate deeply with your subconscious mind, steering your thoughts, beliefs, and actions towards wealth and abundance. Positive affirmations help you visualise the desired outcome, making it easier for your mind to align with the success you seek.

Remember, your words have creative power. By affirming your goals positively, you program your subconscious mind to act in harmony with the life you envision.

"Change your thoughts, and you change your world." - Norman Vincent Peale.

To make your declarations powerful, phrase them in the present tense and in positive language. Instead of saying, "I will be financially free," declare, "I am financially free. I multiply my monthly earnings by 10-fold in passive income." This communicates to your mind that the goal is already a reality in progress. Write these affirmations on cards and place them where you can see them daily—your bathroom mirror, workspace, or even as a screensaver on your devices. Pairing your affirmations with visual representations, like images of your goals, further reinforces their likelihood of manifestation.

> *"Whatever you vividly imagine, ardently desire, sincerely believe, and enthusiastically act upon must inevitably come to pass." — Paul J. Meyer.*

The more you declare your goals, the more you believe in them, and the more likely you are to take inspired actions toward achieving them. Your consistent declarations create a self-fulfilling prophecy, ensuring your words shape your reality.

8. **Create a Clear Plan of Action**
A goal without a plan is just a wish, and the key to turning your desires into reality lies in creating a well-defined roadmap. Start by

setting clear, specific goals using the SMART model: the goals should be Specific, Measurable, Achievable, Relevant, and Time-bound. For example, instead of saying, "I want to save money," a SMART goal would be, "I save 500 dollars monthly for the next 12 months to start a shoe business."

Once your goals are set, break them down into actionable steps. Divide each goal into smaller, manageable tasks with specific deadlines. For instance, if your goal is to write a book, your steps might include creating an outline, writing a chapter per week, and revising within three months. Assign realistic deadlines for each step to ensure steady progress.

> **A goal without a plan is just a wish, and the key to turning your desires into reality lies in creating a well-defined roadmap.**

Celebrate each milestone, no matter how small, as this reinforces your commitment and motivation. For example, finishing the first chapter of your book is an achievement worth acknowledging—it brings you closer to your larger goal.

Additionally, embrace the process, not just the outcome. While reaching your goals is fulfilling, the growth, discipline, and transformation you experience along the journey are equally valuable.

> **Dreams and plans remain stagnant without the power of action.**

"Setting goals is the first step in turning the invisible into the visible."
- Tony Robbins.

9. **Take Action: Put Your Hands to Work**

Dreams and plans remain stagnant without the power of action. While mental preparation lays the foundation for success, it is the physical effort that transforms the ideas into tangible results. You must pair the work of the mind with the labour of the hands. **Simply put, it's not enough to dream of success; you must be willing to act on your dreams.**

Imagine a farmer who envisions a plentiful harvest. He prepares mentally by planning the planting season, selecting quality seeds, and researching the best techniques. However, his vision will never materialise if he doesn't roll up his sleeves to till the soil, plant the seeds, and nurture the crops. Similarly, **your goals require action—a consistent, intentional effort to bring them to life.**

Action is the bridge between where you are and where you want to be. Nothing happens without action, no matter how detailed your plans are or how powerful your affirmations might be.

"The value of an idea lies in the using of it." - Thomas Edison

Your ideas, no matter how brilliant, are worthless unless they are acted upon. Begin now—take the first step, however small, and keep moving forward.

"If you want to change your future, take action and take action now." - Brain Tracy

As we reach the end of this chapter and this book, take a moment to reflect on the journey we've taken together. You've explored the incredible power of your mind—the richest mine—and learned how to uncover and harness its boundless potential. From understanding the immense influence of your thoughts to taking actionable steps toward your dreams, each principle has been a building block for creating the life you envision.

> **Your goals require action—a consistent, intentional effort to bring them to life.**

The journey doesn't stop here. Knowledge is a foundation, but transformation comes from consistent action. As you apply these principles, remember that **success is not an event; it's a process.** Stay patient, persistent, and purposeful, knowing that the seeds you sow today will yield a harvest tomorrow.

> **Action is the bridge between where you are and where you want to be.**

To leverage the richest mine is to embrace your divine potential and courageously craft your destiny. It's about believing that no goal is too lofty and no dream is unattainable.

> *"Go confidently in the direction of your dreams. Live the life you have imagined."* - Henry David Thoreau.

So, **take the first step. Begin where you are, use what you have, and do what you can.** The path may not always be easy, but with faith, focus, and determination, there's no limit to what you can

> **Your ideas, no matter how brilliant, are worthless unless they are acted upon.**

achieve. The richest mine is already within you—now go and make it shine.

I look forward to hearing your success stories and celebrating your achievements with you. Feel free to share your experiences by sending me an email at pnuxelconsulting@gmail.com. Together, let's continue to unlock the treasures within!

> **Take the first step. Begin where you are, use what you have, and do what you can.**

Unlock Your Potential: Discover the Transformative Power of My Other Books

Are you ready to take control of your life and achieve your dreams? Look no further. In addition to **"EXPLORING THE RICHEST MINE: Harnessing the Power Within for Personal, Financial and Professional Success,"** I have also written other books to help guide you on your journey to success.

"FROM OVERWHELMED TO ORGANISED: A Time Management Blueprint for Busy Professionals" reflects an insightful understanding of the challenges those leading demanding professional lives face. Drawing from personal experiences as a busy physician, author, coach, and digital solutions consultant, this book serves as a guide to take you from overwhelmed to organised.

"LEVERAGING THE POWER OF SEASONS: Understanding and Taking Advantage of the Four Seasons of Life" isn't just a book; it's a roadmap to unlocking the treasures and opportunities within the ever-changing seasons of life. This masterpiece will guide you to take advantage of these seasons to achieve great success.

"FIND YOUR WORK: Unlocking Your Path to Impact, Fulfilment, and Worthy Compensation," is a guide to discovering the work you are wired to do, the kind that fills your soul with joy and fulfilment and impacts the world around you. It's about finding fulfilment and earning a worthy reward – not just financial rewards but also the intangible rewards money can't buy. So, if you're tired of feeling trapped in a job that drains you and craves a life of purpose and passion, then this book is for you. Pick up the book and let us find the work that brings joy and fulfilment because life is too short to spend doing anything less

In **"49 Words on Marble,"** I share wisdom and inspiration through powerful affirmations and motivational quotes for men and women, young and old. Positive mindset quotes to start your day and improve your life.

"How to Live Above Circumstances" teaches you how to be in control of your life and overcome any obstacle that may come your way. **"The Beatitudes"** explores the concept of living a life of happiness, prosperity, liberty, and blessedness.

In "**Write a Book Without Breaking a Sweat,**" I share the secrets to writing a book easily, making the process less daunting and more enjoyable. "**The Role of Graphic Design and Technology in Writing**" delves into the blogging world and how to develop a successful blog harnessing technology.

Each of these books offers unique insights and practical advice to help you navigate different aspects of your personal and professional life. Whether you're looking to cultivate a positive mindset, overcome challenges, manage your time effectively, or understand the different seasons of life, there's a book here to support you on your journey.

Take advantage of these transformative books. Check them out today by visiting my website [https://toyinobafemi.com.ng], Amazon store [https://www.amazon.com/Toyin-H.-Obafemi/e/B081TLJKH7], or search for them in your favourite bookstores.

The Author

Dr Toyin Obafemi is an author, coach, and medical doctor, currently serving as a Senior Registrar in Internal Medicine with an interest in Dermatology.

With a commitment to helping people live better lives, Dr Obafemi has authored more than fifteen impactful books published and distributed globally. One of his books, **"From Overwhelmed to Organized: A Time Management Blueprint for Busy Professionals,"** reflects an insightful understanding of the challenges those leading demanding professional lives face. Drawing from personal experiences as a busy physician, author, coach, and digital solutions consultant, this book has earned recognition as an Amazon best-seller.

Having once experienced what it meant to be on an unfulfilling job, Dr Toyin Obafemi understands that the human spirit yearns for something more—something that brings joy and fulfilment. That's why he has written one of his recent books, **"FIND YOUR WORK: Unlocking Your Path to Impact, Fulfilment, and Worthy Compensation,"** to help readers discover the work they are wired to do, the kind that fills their souls with joy and fulfilment. This book is about finding fulfilment and earning worthy rewards—not just financial rewards but also the intangible rewards money can't buy.

Beyond his professional pursuits, Dr Obafemi finds fulfilment in his role as a dedicated spouse to Temitope and a loving father to two children, Oreofe and Inioluwa. This holistic approach to life underscores his value on personal relationships and balance amidst his numerous commitments.

****

Thank you for reading this book. I would love to hear from you. Kindly send your feedback to toyin@toyinobafemi.com.ng or leave me a review at your favourite bookstore. Thanks

****

References

1. Resource curse. In: Wikipedia [Internet]. 2023 [cited 2024 Jan 13]. Available from: https://en.wikipedia.org/w/index.php?title=Resource_curse&oldid=1191997874
2. Japan - Resources, Power, Economy | Britannica [Internet]. [cited 2024 Jan 13]. Available from: https://www.britannica.com/place/Japan/Resources-and-power
3. Economy of Japan. In: Wikipedia [Internet]. 2024 [cited 2024 Jan 13]. Available from: https://en.wikipedia.org/w/index.php?title=Economy_of_Japan&oldid=1195171737
4. Armstrong M, D'Arrigo R, Petter C, Galli A. How resource-poor countries in Asia are securing stable long-term reserves: Comparing Japan's and South Korea's approaches. Resour Policy. 2016 Mar 1;47:51–60.
5. Genesis 1:3 Then God said, "Let there be light"; and there was light. | New King James Version (NKJV) | Download The Bible App Now [Internet]. [cited 2024 Jun 15]. Available from: https://www.bible.com/bible/114/GEN.1.3.NKJV
6. Genesis 1:15 and let them be for lights in the firmament of the heavens to give light on the earth"; and it was so. | New King James Version (NKJV) | Download The Bible App Now [Internet]. [cited 2024 Jun 15]. Available from: https://www.bible.com/bible/114/GEN.1.15.NKJV
7. Genesis 1 NLT [Internet]. [cited 2024 Dec 21]. Available from: https://biblehub.com/nlt/genesis/1.htm

8. Genesis 1:26 Then God said, "Let Us make man in Our image, according to Our likeness; let them have dominion over the fish of the sea, over the birds of the air, and over the cattle, over all the earth and over ev | New King James Version (NKJV) | Download The Bible App Now [Internet]. [cited 2024 Jun 15]. Available from: https://www.bible.com/bible/114/gen.1.26
9. Genesis 1:1 In the beginning God created the heavens and the earth. | New King James Version (NKJV) | Download The Bible App Now [Internet]. [cited 2024 Jun 15]. Available from: https://www.bible.com/bible/114/GEN.1.1.NKJV
10. Proverbs 4:23 Guard your heart above all else, for it determines the course of your life. | New Living Translation (NLT) | Download The Bible App Now [Internet]. [cited 2023 Nov 11]. Available from: https://www.bible.com/bible/116/PRO.4.23.NLT
11. Proverbs 23:7 KJV - For as he thinketh in his heart, so is - Bible Gateway [Internet]. [cited 2024 Dec 21]. Available from: https://www.biblegateway.com/passage/?search=Proverbs%2023%3A7&version=KJV
12. 10 Business Audiobooks to Listen to on Your Commute [Internet]. Investopedia. [cited 2023 Nov 11]. Available from: https://www.investopedia.com/articles/personal-finance/110915/7-business-audiobooks-listen-your-commute.asp
13. Moderate exercise: No pain, big gains - Harvard Health [Internet]. [cited 2023 Nov 11]. Available from: https://www.health.harvard.edu/newsletter_article/Moderate_exercise_No_pain_big_gains
14. Sackton L. 8 Under 8: The Best Audiobooks Under 8 Hours [Internet]. BOOK RIOT. 2020 [cited 2023 Nov 11].

Available from: https://bookriot.com/audiobooks-under-8-hours/
15. Centers SF, Velarde J. Aging Gracefully: The Power of Positive Thinking [Internet]. Senior Friendship Centers. 2023 [cited 2024 Dec 21]. Available from: https://friendshipcenters.org/aging-gracefully-the-power-of-positive-thinking/
16. Shetty M. Optimism as a Means to a Longer Life | Gratitude & Purpose [Internet]. Lifestyle Medicine. 2023 [cited 2024 Dec 21]. Available from: https://longevity.stanford.edu/lifestyle/2023/11/14/optimism-as-a-means-to-a-longer-life/
17. Reader TMP. The New Science of Optimism and Longevity [Internet]. The MIT Press Reader. 2024 [cited 2024 Dec 21]. Available from: https://thereader.mitpress.mit.edu/the-new-science-of-optimism-and-longevity/
18. Deuteronomy 8.18 (KJV) [Internet]. [cited 2024 Dec 21]. Available from: https://legacy.biblesociety.org.uk/explore-the-bible/read/eng/KJV/Deut/8/18/
19. Acts 8:30-31 The Spirit told Philip, "How can I, unless someone guides me?" And he invited Philip to come up [Internet]. [cited 2024 Dec 21]. Available from: https://www.bible.com/bible/compare/ACT.8.30-31
20. Joshua 13:1 [cited 2024 Dec 21]. Available from: https://www.bible.com/bible/compare/JOS.13.1
21. John 9:4 I must work the works of Him who sent Me while it is day; the night is coming when no one can work. | New King James Version (NKJV) | Download The Bible App Now [Internet]. [cited 2024 Jun 15]. Available from: https://www.bible.com/bible/114/JHN.9.4.NKJV

22. Jeremiah 29:11 - For I know the plans I have for you," declares the... [Internet]. [cited 2024 Dec 21]. Available from: https://www.biblestudytools.com/jeremiah/29-11.html
23. Isaiah 55:8-9 "For my thoughts are not your thoughts, neither are your ways my ways," declares the LORD. "As the heavens are higher than the earth, so are my ways higher than your ways and my thoughts than your tho | New International Version (NIV) | Download The Bible App Now [Internet]. [cited 2024 Dec 21]. Available from: https://www.bible.com/bible/111/ISA.55.8-9.NIV

www.ingramcontent.com/pod-product-compliance
Lightning Source LLC
Chambersburg PA
CBHW031616210526
45464CB00004B/1608